The Weste

A Postcard Tour

---

1. Barra to North Uist

Bob Charnley

HEBRIDEAN IMAGES

www.hebrideanimages.com

First published in the United Kingdom in 1992
by MacLean Press
60 Aird Bhearnasdail, by Portree, Isle of Skye

This Edition published in 2007
by Hebridean Images
5 East Kilbride, Lochboisdale, Isle of South Uist, H58 5TS
Tel: 01878 700 573
hebrideanimages@btinternet.com

ISBN 978 0 9555108 0 9

Design Layout by MacLean Press and Adlard Print
Printed by Adlard Print & Reprographics Ltd., The Old School, The Green,
Ruddington, Notts. NG11 6HH Tel: (0115) 921 4663 www.adlardprint.com

CONTENTS:

"The sea is all islands, and the land all lakes;
that which is not rock is sand,
and that which is not mud is bog,
and that which is not bog is lake,
and that which is not lake is sea!"

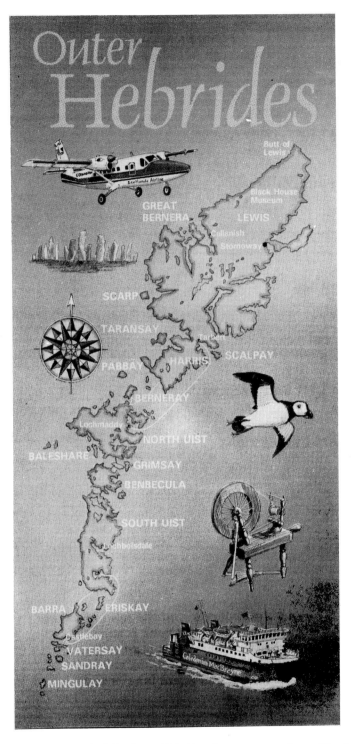

A popular, modern postcard of the Outer Hebrides; from a range of over 50 colourful Long Island cards produced by Charles Tait of St. Ola, Orkney.

4

PREFACE

"Sweet loving-kindness! If thou shine,
The plainest face may seem divine,
And beauty's self grow doubly bright
In the mild glory of thy light."

Much of my early childhood was spent in the English Lake District, around Ambleside, Rydal and Grasmere, where the tarns sparkled all summer, the streams yielded up their sticklebacks and the mountains dwarfed my lonely, childish games.

Even before my eighteenth birthday, I had experienced cold fear within the Coliseum of Rome and found total peace in a beautiful Florentine garden; seen all of the sectors of the city of Berlin *before* the infamous Wall, and photographed Lapps in the wastes of the Arctic Circle. But Scotland, although never more than eighty miles or so away, was unvisited, and not until the late 1960s did I personally 'discover' the Highlands and Islands.

Today, one can linger in solitude or savour great communal warmth in these islands, but the terrible happenings of the past, when many of the islanders were driven to despair, poverty, hunger and eventual banishment from the very land you walk upon, should never be too far from your thoughts.

For many years I have collected images and ephemera of these islands and this book contains my selection, chosen from an accumulation of thousands of early photos, picture postcards and documents. Space does not permit me to share everything, and deciding what had to be left out was difficult. I believe the balance is about right, but it generally reflects the type and availability of particular postcards in the islands over a forty year period. Some districts are not featured; the postcard-photographers may have neglected to visit the area or the picture has not yet been 'discovered', but I do hope you will enjoy this nostalgic photographic tour around parts of beautiful Barra, Eriskay, South Uist, Benbecula and North Uist. Do remember, it was *all so very long ago* and you will notice many changes!

Bob Charnley
November 1992

BEHIND THE CAMERA LENS

For more than twenty years I have been adding items to an ever-growing accumulation of books, ephemera and photographic images of the Western Highlands and Islands of Scotland. Today this personal collection contains much varied material, but from the very first moments of the 'chase' one particular group of exclusively Hebridean photographs stood out - head and shoulders above all the rest.

Reproduced as postcards - which I will call the *Cairt Phostail* series or images - and printed by Philip G. Hunt of Deansgate in Manchester, with a later reprint in Berlin, the photographs were taken in the Outer Isles of Barra, Eriskay, South Uist, Benbecula, North Uist, Berneray and Harris, sometime around and between the 1890s and early 1900s. *(illustration I)* Without exception every card has the wording on the address side in Gaelic *(illustration II)*, whereas the caption on the view side is usually in English, and of the 136 cards discovered so far all but ten have the word *'Copyright'* next to the title.

Iasgairachd. (Copyright.)

A Gaelic series *Cairt Phostail* showing young Hebridean fishermen. This photograph, with the English title **'Boys Fishing, Uist'**, was used in October 1903 on a postcard issued to publicize the attendance of the Scottish Home Industries Association at a two day exhibition in Manchester *(Illustration 66)*.

And herein lies the mystery! Just who was 'Behind the Camera Lens' at the end of the last century, claiming copyright to these excellent, late Victorian/early Edwardian photographs?

No credit, acknowledgement or trade-mark appears on the cards, yet they were most definitely *not* the work of some city-dwelling tourist, wandering aimlessly through an alien landscape hardly understanding one word being said about him behind his back. Perhaps a Victorian English gentleman might have felt at home in the warmth and comfort of the Lochmaddy Hotel talking of fishing, but certainly not standing with herring-gutters in Castlebay or walking behind a plough in South Uist.

On and off over the years I tried to identify the photographer, but those part-time efforts always came to naught and I allowed the trail to go cold; until 1991, when a little piece of good fortune came my way.

In April that year a collection of postcards came up for auction at Christie's in Glasgow and all the cards were from the Gaelic *Cairt Phostail* series - apart from one 'rogue' card of which more later. The postcards were in mint unused condition with much duplication, which suggested that it was remaindered stock that had been stored away in some dark corner for the best part of sixty years.

Back in the early 1970s, when Francis Thompson wrote **'The Uists and Barra'** for publisher David & Charles, he included a few of these early views of the islands in the book and credited them to a *'Mrs. Cathcart of Inverness'*. Finding and talking to the Cathcart family was now an urgent priority and I set off along the trail once again.

In 1964 Mrs. Margaret Cathcart, then of 33 Kenneth Street, Inverness, donated an assorted group of some sixty original photographs to the Royal Museum of Scotland. Now referred to as the *'Cathcart Collection'* and held in the Scottish Ethnological Archive in Queen Street, Edinburgh, the pictures vary in size and quality, and whilst some have an exact location and date inscribed on the reverse the majority carry no information, though on close examination it is obvious that all of the photographs are of people and places in the Outer Isles.

CAIRT PHOSTAIL.

CUIR AN SEOLADH AIR AN TAOBH SEO.

CEUD-BHEATH D'N EILEAN-FHAD

Pictorial Post Cards, Platinum, (as this sample.)

Produced from Customers' Originals. (P.O.P. Prints preferred.)

	Per 500 each.	Per 1000 each.	Per 2000 each
Single subjects	12/-	20/-	18/-
Six „	11/-	16/6	16/6
Twelve „	10/6	15/6	16/-
Twenty five „	10/-	15/-	14/6

SPECIAL QUOTATIONS FOR LARGER QUANTITIES.

PHILIP G. HUNT, Pictorial Post Card Printer,

November, 1904.   100, Deansgate, MANCHESTER.

The reverse of the *Cairt Phostail* of Lochmaddy *(illustration 121)*, used by the printer Philip Hunt of Manchester to advertise his prices for producing postcards for the trade. The card was useful as a guide to the period of this particular Gaelic series; it bears the printed date *'November, 1904'*.

Fortunately, postcards in the *Cairt Phostail* series had been produced from some of the same negatives and we now know that the unidentified photograph in the *Cathcart Collection* - archive reference number 1735 - was taken in Castlebay, Barra. *(illustration 6)*

But linking the *Cairt Phostail* images with the photographs in the *Cathcart Collection* did not identify the photographer and the Cathcart family were unable to offer any further help; Margaret Cathcart bought the photos at a local jumble sale many years ago and never knew the identity of the actual donor. The door was firmly closed on that line of enquiry.

However all was not lost, for amongst the *Cairt Phostail* items in the Christie's sale there was still that one 'rogue' card mentioned earlier. With English instead of Gaelic on the reverse side, the postcard shows a line of children in the snow outside Ostrom House, Lochmaddy, and printed alongside the picture, the 1906 Christmas greetings of *'Mr. and Mrs. Chisholm'*. A new name and a possible clue to investigate *(illustration III).*

The 1906 Christmas postcard of Archibald and Helen Chisholm of Ostrom House, Lochmaddy. The children playing in the snow outside Ostrom are, from left to right, Flora Chisholm age 13, her sisters Helen, 10, Mary, 6, and their brother Aeneas, age 9 years. Their former home is now the Lochmaddy Youth Hostel. [Black and white printed postcard].

Known today as *Ostram* House or the Lochmaddy Youth Hostel, at the beginning of the century Ostram was an imposing, Estate-owned, private property used by His Majesty's Procurator-Fiscal of the Long Island District of Inverness-shire, and in 1906 the resident Fiscal was Archibald Alexander Chisholm, born in Kiltarlity near Beauly in January 1859 to Flora and Aeneas Chisholm.

In July 1892, 33 year-old Archibald Chisholm married Helen Annie McHardy, the 24 year-old daughter of Alexander McHardy, later Lt. Col. Sir Alexander McHardy C.B., K.C.B., the wedding taking place in the Catholic church of St. Margaret's in Kinning Park, Glasgow.

The couple were to be blessed with six children - Flora, born in Inverness in 1893, Helen in 1896 and Aeneas in 1897. The fourth child, Mary, was born in 1900 in Lochmaddy, but her sister Margaret must have arrived unexpectedly early - her birthplace is shown as the Portree Hotel, Skye, on New Year's Day, 1903. One can only imagine the joyous, extra celebrations of the family, staff and guests that day! The last child, Archibald, was born in Lochmaddy in 1904.

Wrestling with the roots of this unfamiliar genealogical tree, I spent many hours on the telephone talking to friends and total strangers in Berneray, Edinburgh, Furnace, Glasgow, Inverness, Kiltarlity, Lerwick, Lochmaddy, Newton Ferry, Portree and Stornoway, and I am indebted to each and everyone of them; they were all *very* tolerant of my questioning. I was passed between friends and strangers, from office to Court, Fiscal to Sheriff, and between countless number of Chisholms throughout Inverness-shire, and the snippets of information that they supplied finally brought me into direct contact with the one person who could answer all my questions.

Miss Josephine Chisholm, a cousin of the former Lochmaddy Procurator-Fiscal, sketched for me in words, a wonderful portrait of the 'tall, bulky man' whom she had met in the thirites when she was a very young child, and she was able to confirm my suspicions that Chisholm - Archie to his friends - was both Fiscal and photographer in North Uist. Miss Chisholm explained how all his remaining stock of *Cairt Phostail* images came into her possession and hinted at the whereabouts of the original glass-plates; they were sold separately in the 1940s to a gentleman living in a village along-side the A9 and may still be with the family in -- but no, that's another story!

Archibald Alexander Chisholm's undisputed right to be recognized and remembered as the man 'Behind the Camera Lens' is now revealed, publicly, for the first time.

'*Rhuiar'*, Lochmaddy, as it looked in August 1992. On the right, the remains of Sponish House, the residence of the Sheriff in Chisholm's day. *(Illustration 116).*

It was Chisholm who took the *Cathcart Collection* photographs, now in the Scottish Ethnological Archives in Edinburgh, and it was Chisholm who held the copyright for all the Hebridean picture postcards in the *Cairt Posthail* series. His photographic contribution to Scotland's heritage may be small and localized when compared to that of Photographer-Royal for Scotland, George Washington Wilson, but it is all the greater for it and his name can now be written into the record books.

But life was not easy in the Hebrides, and whilst Archie Chisholm, *photographer,* enjoyed his excursions between Lochmaddy and Castlebay, Archibald Alexander Chisholm, *Procurator-Fiscal,* was having a difficult time in North Uist with the owner of the island, Sir John William Powlett Campbell Orde of Kilmory and North Uist, Baronet, (1827-1897), their relationship being nothing if not tempestuous.

In October 1890 Chisholm was served with a 'Notice to Remove' from the property of *'Rhuiar'* in Lochmaddy - a house he had occupied since 1882 and which he described as being *"small, old and rickety"* - and from the land formerly known as the croft of James Macdonald, both properties being owned by Sir John Orde. Even without the benefit of a Victorian *West Highland Free Press*, the news spread almost as quickly amongst the crofters in Barra, Eriskay and the Uists[1] as it does today; their Procurator-Fiscal was being evicted! *(illustration IV)* Lengthy and acrimonious correspondence then passed between landlord and tenant, some letters being sent personally between the two men but most going through their respective legal agents.

Orde chose Messrs Tods, Murray & Jamieson, W.S., of Queen Street, Edinburgh, a firm with considerable experience in dealing with such matters, having previously advised the trustees of the Waterstein estate in Skye during their *'troubles'* with the crofters in the 1880s.

Chisholm however needed someone more accessible and he called upon his friend Thomas Wilson, who had arrived in Lochmaddy as a 26 year-old solicitor in 1882 - the year after Chisholm - and was a popular and well-respected figure with the crofters in Barra, Eriskay and the Uists. Some twelve years later, Wilson was asked about his experiences in dealing with the people in the islands.

"I have been through their homes in every district", he replied proudly. "I have travelled on foot through almost every inch of the Long Island, time after time. I have been in crofters' houses, and cottars' houses, and houses of every description, and have been constantly among the people, and I should say that I know them as well as any man at the present day. I have a very high opinion of the people of these islands; they are a very law-abiding and a very moral people".

Wilson willingly took up the cudgels on behalf of his client, relishing, for personal reasons which will become obvious shortly, every opportunity to challenge the authority of Orde.

In June 1894 Wilson spoke publicly about himself, Chisholm and Orde, when the Royal Commission visited Lochmaddy whilst investigating the effects of the Crofters Act on certain aspects of life in the Outer Isles.

"And what, in your judgement, is the reason for Sir John Orde having such an aversion to the settlement of crofters here?" Wilson was asked by the Chairman of the Royal Commission, George Gordon.

"He is different from almost any man I have ever met in my life," he replied. "He is one of those peculiar men whom no one understands; what his reasons are I cannot tell you, and I don't suppose anybody else could. I think he scarcely knows himself!"

Gordon then asked Wilson if he thought that former North Uist men, who had gone to the south to work, would like to return to the island and build homes. He replied that he had no doubts that they would.

"And are there instances of their being refused?" pressed Gordon.

"Yes, I have known instances of their being refused, and not only those from the south," retorted Wilson. "I myself have been refused, and the Procurator-Fiscal has been refused a site. We are both without a house at the present day, compelled to trust to the generosity of friends for lodgings. We have been so situated for years, and can scarcely carry on our public duties for the want of a house."

In revealing his own lack of accommodation, Wilson played a winning card. Privately, the four individual members of the Commission knew of his plight, but since it was now public knowledge it could only embarrass Orde, and in all future dealings on Chisholm's behalf Wilson would be remembered as an equally aggrieved and injured party. Quite obviously neither Fiscal nor solicitor was popular with the owner of North Uist.

---

[1]The phrase 'The Uists' is a space-saver and I apologize for using it; I dislike it too! In this book 'The Uists' refers to South Uist, Benbecula, North Uist and Berneray. No correspondence please!

In **'The Crofters' War'** (Acair, 1989), Dr. I.M.M. MacPhail writes - tantalisingly briefly - of the declining relationship between crofter and proprietor in North Uist after the passing of the 1886 Crofters Act, a piece of legislation which was distinctly not to Orde's liking. He constantly objected when his tenants applied to the Crofters Commission for fixed fair rents and did everything in his power, lawful and otherwise, to harass them. In 1887 one crofter, Donald MacLellan of Tigharry, argued his case to the satisfaction of the Crofters Commission and it over-ruled the Lochmaddy Sheriff Court order that his effects be sold. Orde was furious and he struck out - not at the crofter who had dared to challenge him but at his legal agent, Thomas Wilson, and a very clear message was sent by Orde to all his tenants; Wilson was not to be given lodgings in North Uist. Yet seven years later here he was, still in Lochmaddy and still defending the right of the individual to be housed, be it a Procurator-Fiscal or a crofter.

The next question from the Chairman on that June day in 1894 appears, now, to have been particularly loaded but he was finding it difficult to hide his sympathies:

"Don't you think *that* is a serious disadvantage; that people cannot get sites for their houses on reasonable terms?"

"I think it is very serious. I think it strikes at the foundation of all justice," answered Wilson forcefully, ever mindful that all his remarks were being recorded by William McKenzie, the Secretary to the Royal Commission, and would eventually be presented to both Houses of Parliament as *Minutes of Evidence.*

"If justice is to be administered in this island impartially," he added, "I think it only right that the Procurator-Fiscal, who is the Crown public prosecutor for the Inverness-shire portion of the Outer Hebrides with a population of 20,000, and every other public official, should have an independent home."

"And is it the case that the proprietor of this island refuses to give sites for houses in every case, except where he is compelled by some Act of Parliament?" queried Gordon.

"I know that, so far as individuals are concerned, there is no instance where a feu or lease has been granted for a dwelling house," answered Wilson.

Henry Munro, a member of the Royal Commission sitting alongside the Chairman, had a few observations of his own that day:

"I should also like, Mr. Chairman, to express my own mind and opinion on this matter. Certainly, very grave charges have been made against the management of Sir John Orde's estate, but whether Mr. Orde is in a position to repudiate any of these charges or to give us any additional information is more than I can say. Still, I am bound to say this much, that I consider it exceedingly unfortunate indeed that there is no person here appearing today in the interests of Sir John's estates."

Wilson then introduced into evidence copies of all the correspondence relating to the eviction of Chisholm by Sir John Orde. Published in full in Volume II of the *'Minutes of Evidence, Royal Commission (Highlands and Islands, 1892)'*, the letters reveal something of Chisholm's attitude towards Orde and his determined refusal to be intimidated.

"You are aware that to evict me now from the only available dwelling-house forces me to break up my home, and displenish my furniture stock &c., and thus I will be put to serious inconvenience and loss" he wrote to Orde in November, 1891. *"I regret exceedingly that I must at last take a stand and say I will pay only what is legally due ..."*

And in a letter to Tods, Murray & Jamieson dated December of that same year, Chisholm remarked about Orde's personal attitude towards himself:

"Why, when I met him on the public road here (in Lochmaddy), and approached him with the intention of speaking to him, did he in the presence of the Sheriff-Substitute, turn his back on me?"

Tods, Murray & Jamieson replied to Chisholm but merely repeated Orde's demand regarding an amount of rent, still allegedly unpaid but strenuously disputed by Chisholm.

However, the Procurator-Fiscal was not to be bullied. In 1892 he had married the daughter of an important Chief Constable, been accepted as a member of the Gaelic society of Inverness, and was fully prepared for battle, confident in the knowledge that influential people supported his stance.

"It is time an end should be put to the position into which the Public Prosecutor for the district has been driven," he wrote in March 1893, *"and of being without a dwelling house of his own to reside in, and indebted for hospitality to a local gentleman - not even being permitted to live in the only hotel in the place, the property of Sir John ..."*

Chisholm also encountered a personal problem with Orde's legal agent in Edinburgh, and writing to Tods, Murray & Jamieson in November 1893 he complained:

"I ought in fairness to you to candidly say that the dual position of your Mr. Jamieson, as Crown Agent for Scotland (through whose office my official correspondence had for years passed), and as private agent for Sir John Orde, has to my mind been, in these proceedings, an unsatisfactory factor ..."

Wilson had a similar complaint, but in his case the person holding the *'dual position'* was none other than the Lord Advocate for Scotland, Sir Charles Pearson, who, when addressing the House of Commons on matters relating to crofters in the isles, used information supplied by Orde. But the Lord Advocate was also retained by Orde as his own, paid, private counsel and the facts given to him were, allegedly, biased and of a dubious nature.

Just four months before the arrival of the Royal Commission Wilson sent his final letter, dated February 1894, to Tods, Murray & Jamieson:

"... I see from the 'Northern Chronicle' that your client, Sir John Orde, was on the 5th ulto. at the Central Hotel, Glasgow," he wrote, *"and was then offering to travel to Inverness if someone else would pay his expenses, so that your excuse for him of ill-health comes to me very much like the echo of the reason given for his failure to proceed beyond Varna, when his country's battles had to be fought in the Crimea."*

Having made this potentially libellous comment, presumably on his *own* behalf rather than Chisholm's - and some forty years after the alleged event when Orde had been a Captain in the 42nd Foot - Wilson continued:

"I was struck with the conduct of your client, Sir John Orde, in systematically blackmailing and outrageously evicting Her Majesty's Procurator-Fiscal in these islands, and refusing him a place of abode anywhere 'in North Uist', ostensibly over a trifling matter of a few pounds, but, as is now clear, really because he did his public duty justly and fearlessly over the whole area of his jurisdiction; and would not make any exception 'in North Uist' ..."

Whilst this is strong language - even for a solicitor - Wilson must have felt that he was on very firm ground and could finally expose Orde's perceived attempt to influence the judgement of the Procurator-Fiscal. Warming to his task he continued:

"It is too monstrous for expression to find (as the correspondence clearly shows, has been Mr. Chisholm's experience at Sir John Orde's hands) that in the 19th century, the Crown Public Prosecutor should not dare impartially to perform the public duties he is sworn to perform without having the wrath and systematic vengeance of the man who happens to be sole proprietor of North Uist Island levelled at him."

Towards the close of his lengthy letter Wilson again referred to Chisholm's main complaint - his lack of accommodation in Lochmaddy:

"Evicted from his own home through your agency on a trumped up pretext, which I observe you afterwards not only abandoned, but desired even to drop discussion of; his household effects compelled to be sacrificed by sale at public auction; thereafter a pretence of willingness to re-let, which, when examined, was seen to be a pettifogging dodge. Next, the only hotel in the place - also belonging to Sir John Orde - debarred him; every harassment studiously used against him, and he himself forced to trust to the generosity of the only leaseholder in the district for a roof over the heads of himself and his family." Then with one final threat he concluded:

"It is deplorably humiliating to find that in that course of outrageous conduct Sir

John Orde has been aided by the Crown Agent for Scotland for pay. I propose present-
ing a petition to Her Majesty the Queen in Council in regard to this matter."

This insight into the dispute between Orde and Chisholm is a matter of public record. What really sparked off the row - and it is my opinion that it was definitely something *other* than the alleged unpaid rent - is either forgotten or was never pub-licly revealed; then again, perhaps their personal secret is still concealed within a file, hidden deep in the basement of an office somewhere in Edinburgh.

Sir John Orde died in October 1897; Ostrom House was subsequently leased by the Estate for the use of the resident Procurator-Fiscal - until the mid-1950s - and Tho-mas Wilson finally got his house. Just before the outbreak of the Great War, Archie Chisholm left Lochmaddy to take up an appointment as Sheriff Clerk in Inverness where he died in 1933, and for the purposes of this book that is almost the end of the matter. But mention must be made of one final, ironic occurrence.

Many years later, Margaret Chisholm - the 1903 New Year's Day birthday-girl - decided to follow in her father's footsteps. In the 1940s she was appointed Deputy Sheriff Clerk - in Lochmaddy! How proud and how fortunate she was; she got to stay in the hotel that had been barred to her father in the 1890s - the Lochmaddy Hotel!

After World War I many more tourists boarded ships in Liverpool, Glasgow and Oban and headed for the Scottish islands. With them came the demands, the very least being a more up-to-date selection of postcards, thus Archie Chisholm's *Cairt Phostail* images, some now 25 years old and from a very different era, were gradually replaced.

Thanks to the efforts of a group of freelance photographers working for the *Scholas-tic Souvenir Company* of Bispham, Blackpool, a new range of 'Real Photographic' post-cards appeared on the market and many of their island views can also be found within this book. Different trade-marks were used by this Lancashire firm to identify their cards, but in common with many other publishers the *Scholastic Souvenir Company* failed to mark all their postcards, and examples of their work must still lie, unrecog-nized, in albums and cardboard boxes throughout the kingdom. *(illustration V)* More details of this company and its founder Yorkshireman Willie Binns can be found in **'Skye: A Postcard Tour'** (Maclean Press 1992).

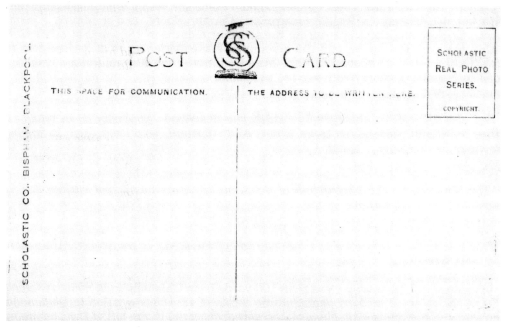

The reverse side of a real photographic postcard view of Lochboisdale, produced by the *Scholastic Souve-nir Company* of Bispham, Blackpool, in the 1920s. Many variations of the company logo were used during the life-time of this firm.

Whilst I re-used my rusting skills of *sleuthing* to unmask the Tunbridge Wells doctor Francis Gray Smart, and identify him as the Victorian photographer of Glenelg in Inverness-shire (**'The Summer of '89'**, Maclean Press 1991), detection was never the ultimate purpose of this book. The first volume of the Western Isles Postcard Tour is primarily a presentation of sheer nostalgia and a tribute to all photographers, known or anonymous, who with camera on tripod and in hand moved around the isles between the 1880s and the 1930s, recording the people, their homes, work-places and environment.

Many fine photographs have been taken in these islands since the end of World War II - I think especially of the contribution made by Kenneth Robertson; the *'Scots Magazine'* and *'Scotland's Magazine'* never seemed to be without his pictures in the 1960s - and I hope that the local history societies will continue to look towards the future and add more images to their collections, following the splendid example set by *Comann Eachdraidh Uibhist a Tuath.*

Some of the sites and old buildings have altered little over the years whilst others - Eoligarry House in Barra for example - have gone forever; and as we approach the 21st century any alteration seems to be so immediate that the *old* demands to be equally well recorded on negative before the *new* takes over.

Obvious changes, from Castlebay to Lochmaddy and beyond, are the latest piers, built specifically for the present generation of roll-on/roll-off Cal-Mac ferries; but just as noticeable are those extra 'bits' that have been added on to some of the older hotels and crofts. And then there are the *'Passing Places'* - constantly disappearing as they are swallowed up by the wider, straighter roads which ease our progress through the isles at speeds we should not really reach! I wonder, how much of the landscape do any of us actually see at sixty miles an hour? But perhaps we should be watching out for the sheep on the road anyway.

Within the caption to some of the photographs you will read comments made by many previous travellers who moved around the islands at a more leisurely pace; in particular, the remarks made by a certain Miss Ada Goodrich-Freer, a lady whose name might not be too familiar.

Leaving the Victorian comfort of her London home the young Miss Goodrich-Freer - with her dog 'Scamp', a female companion, Connie Moore, and a *camera* - visited Barra, Eriskay and the Uists during the summer months of 1894 and at other times within the next few years, and the account of her experiences is to be found in the book **'Outer Isles'**, published in 1902. Miss Goodrich-Freer also undertook investigations into matters concerning psychic phenomena, using her tour of the islands to compile material for articles and lectures relating to second-sight which she wrote or delivered later.

Her own Hebridean photographs, which she described - modestly or in truth - as being *'imperfect'*, were given to an artist, Allan Baraud, who used them to produce drawings for her book, though there are less than a dozen of Barra, Eriskay or the Uists within the 448 pages. And yet Miss Goodrich-Freer refers to an eviction in North Uist, which she witnessed, and of which she wrote:

"The time came - the photograph of the scene is in my possession - when her few belongings were turned out by the roadside, and she herself laid upon the miserable bedding which, with a wooden chest, a couple of chairs, a single cooking pot, a few bits of crockery, constituted her entire wealth."

This throw-away reference to a *'photograph of the scene'* is particularly interesting and most intriguing.

Some years ago, whilst staying with Margaret and Norman Johnson at the Old Court House in Lochmaddy - less than 100 yards from Chisholm's old home at Ostrom - I was shown some modern photographic copies of an 1890s eviction in Lochmaddy. The original, half-plate size, glass plates were discovered in the loft of the Lochmaddy bank house but the identity of the photographer was never known, although when Francis Thompson reproduced one of the pictures in his **'Victorian and Edwardian Highlands from old Photographs'** (Batsford, 1976), he wrote that it was *'suspected* *with reasonable grounds'* that Miss Goodrich-Freer was responsible and I have never wanted to challenge that assertion - until now!

Seventeen years later, and with the added benefit of fresh evidence, I believe that there are good reasons for finding Miss Goodrich-Freer innocent.

First, I do not believe that the lady ever carried a heavy, brass-bound, mahogany half-plate field camera and tripod around Barra, Eriskay and the Uists when the new range of light-weight, hand-held, quarter-plate cameras was so readily available.

Second, Miss Goodrich-Freer had her home in London in the 1890s, and unless she was extremely careless and forgot her glass-plates, they should have been discovered hundreds of miles away in England instead of in a building just yards from the actual eviction site in Lochmaddy.

Third, and more important, within the *Cathcart Collection* there are seven similar Lochmaddy eviction photographs (archive reference 1707, 1711-12 & 4301-4), and I suggest that it was someone living locally, with *inside information,* who took all those poignant, pathetic eviction photographs.

Someone who knew the exact day, time and place of all Lochmaddy evictions; someone who very conveniently just happened to have a camera already set upon its tripod, glass plates prepared and loaded in their slides; someone angered by Sir John Orde's method of dealing with those who opposed him; someone who cared not a jot that his attendance at the scene - with a camera - would be unwelcome; someone who wanted evidence that could be used to embarrass the landowner if it were ever necessary, and I know of no worthier suspect than the evicted Procurator-Fiscal himself, photographer Archie Chisholm.

What Miss Goodrich-Freer wrote in **'Outer Isles'** was that *"the photograph of the scene is in my possession",* but she did not use the image in the book nor did she actually claim to be the photographer, and with the evidence of Chisholm's own Lochmaddy eviction photos in the *Cathcart Collection* it is very possible that he supplied her with one of his own prints a day or two after the event.

Ada Goodrich-Freer may not have been much of an expert with the camera but she was still an observant traveller. Her account of what she saw and how she felt is included as her comments are relevant; Miss Goodrich-Freer was writing about the islands at the same moment in time that Archie Chisholm was taking his photographs. Despite all the criticisms made of her I have included her contemporary remarks and they are identified by her initials [G-F].

Do not be offended by her words; she was often appalled by what she saw. She was also very conscious of the circumstances that had brought about the suffering and misery of the people in the islands and said so in her book.

Postcard-photographers - aware of the growing commercial market - recorded the pleasing aspects of Hebridean life, ignoring the poverty, sickness and hardship of the people in the interests of a saleable item. Miss Goodrich-Freer had no such considerations; she wrote it as she saw it. *All of it, thankfully, relates to a time that has now passed and in no way must it be compared to the present day life-style in these islands.*

Incidentally, whilst indulging his passion for sailing, that Oxford academic and keen yachtsman C.C. Lynam, M.A., also visited these islands; in August 1902 he sailed into Lochboisdale and his 300 page tome, **The Log of the 'Blue Dragon' 1892-1904',** records the event:

"We anchored off the pier in Loch Boisdale and had an excellent soup. Then skipper went ashore for letters, and amongst other things got Miss Freer's book on the Outer Isles". A good few years later, whilst indulging *my* passion, I attended a major postcard fair in York and from amongst the thousands of old cards I recovered the 1911 postcard shown here. *(illustration VI)*

Other comments within the captions are mine and I accept full responsibility for them, but the varieties of spelling on the actual picture postcards - particularly in Gaelic - are by someone from the distant past and will undoubtedly amuse, and even confuse, some of my Gaelic-speaking friends. A few cards have their own quite peculiar variations which may not be identical with the modern version - but whether it be Dalabrog, Dhalibrog or Daliburgh is not too important, as long as you can identify and locate the area from one of the versions.

But let none of this mar the pleasure of your wanderings from Barra to Eriskay and across to South Uist, Benbecula, North Uist and Berneray; this is a *nostalgic* trip intended to take you back to a time that *"was all so very long ago"*. Enjoy the pictures and remember that things may look a little different today but what changes will the *next* generation make in these islands?

Wishing you
the Compliments
of the Season.

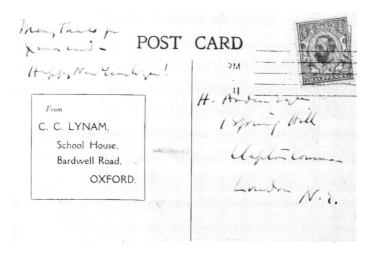

Both sides of yachtsman C.C. Lynam's Christmas and New Year postcard for the year 1911. Discovered at a postcard fair in York, at just 20p it proved to be an unusual but worthy addition to the author's Western Isles collection.

BARRA
Eilean Barraigh

"An island of the Outer Hebrides, Inverness-shire. It has a post office with money order and savings bank departments; a ferry boat, with the mails, plies twice a week from Polochar Inn, South Uist, and a weekly steamer calls at Bayherivagh and Castlebay. Fishing banks extend from Loch Boisdale to Barra Head and give a great yield of cod and ling. So many as about 80 boats, manned by 400 hands belonging to the parish, are usually employed in the fishery. Frequent communication is maintained by boats or small vessels with the Clyde. A cattle fair is held on the Friday before the third Wednesday in July, and on the Friday in September before South Uist. The property all belonged to the McNeills from time immemorial till 1840, was then sold to Colonel Gordon of Cluny, and now belongs to Sir Reginald Cathcart, Bart. Population 2131" *(Extract (part) from Volume I, 'Ordnance Gazetteer of Scotland: A Survey of Scottish Topography, Statistical, Biographical and Historical.' New Edition c. 1895).*

Castlebay. (Copyright.)

1. *"Barra has quite enough to endure without the invasion of the tourist."* These words from Ada Goodrich-Freer's book **'Outer Isles'**, form part of her opening remarks on arriving at Castlebay. It is to the benefit of the 20th century traveller that the majority of the people on the island of Barra might disagree with the remark, made in the 1890s. This view of **Castlebay** - *Bagh A Chaisteil* - must have been most welcoming to Ada after her seven and a half hour voyage from Oban, and time has not diminished that feeling of anticipation - for *this* particular passenger anyway - when the pier is reached today. The small islet of Oronsay, right of centre, was linked by a foot-bridge at this time and the substantial buildings visible in this photograph were the curing-stations for the busy Victorian herring industry. Only the extensive foundations remain today. [A Gaelic series, black and white printed *Cairt Phostail circa* 1902, photo *circa* 1897]

2. Bagh a' Chaisteil, Barraigh; Castlebay harbour, and the fishing fleet is on the move. *"None of the Islands has an approach half so picturesque as that of Castle Bay, nor such an air, fictitious though it be, of prosperity and well-being."* [G-F] A modern roll-on, roll-off pier stands alongside the old, much improved landing-stage, which served the fishing boats well but was not built to cope with the volume of traffic which now arrives on board the large, 20th century ferries in particular *'Lord of the Isles'*. Relax over a coffee in the sun-lounge of the Castlebay Hotel and compare this picture with the present view; the island police-station and house now dominates the foreground, whilst the barrels and sheds of the defunct fishing industry have been replaced by an assortment of buildings and store-places. [A Gaelic series, black and white printed *Cairt Phostail circa* 1902, photo *circa* 1897]

3. A late 1920s view of **Kisimul Castle.** An early fortification of disputed age with tradition dating it to the 11th century though the 13th century is more likely. It was not until the mid-15th century that all the additions were made, including a kitchen, chapel and galley-crew house. The building suffered greatly from vandalism in the mid-1800s and nothing of the two-storey crew house remains, much of the stone having been taken for ballast or as material for some of the larger properties on Barra isle itself. Thanks to the efforts of the 45th Chief of Clan Neil, Robert Lister Macneil, who purchased the Estate of Barra in 1937, the castle is no longer a ruin and American-born Ian Roderick, the present Macneil of Barra, continues the never-ending process of maintenance and restoration, encouraging the summer visitor to visit his famed 'Castle in the Sea'. [Real photographic postcard by the *Scholastic Souvenir Company* of Blackpool, *circa* 1928]

4. *"Entering Castle Bay, if it be in the early summer, we may be surprised at the bustle and business going on, the place being, during May and June, a kind of herring metropolis."* Castlebay was perhaps the best centre for the west coast herring industry at this time, and **Fraser's Curing Station** was but one of over forty such premises scattered around the bay. It was common practice, at the start of the season, for the skippers of the fishing boats to meet with the representatives of the curing-stations and hammer out a 'fair-deal' agreement, whereby a boat would remain under contract to the same fish-curer. *"The shores are lined with heaps of herring-barrels, and the bay bristles with 'sixerns' from all parts, and little boats, amid which are two or three steamers waiting their freights."* **(Baddeley's Guide to Scotland 1908 edition).** [Black and white printed card with undivided back, publisher unidentified, *circa* 1899. This example posted from Castlebay, July 1903]

KISIMUL CASTLE, CASTLEBAY.

5 & 6. Fisher Girls usually worked in teams of three, the tallest girl being chosen to do the packing as she could always reach the bottom of the barrel! The other pair did the really dirty work - beheading, gutting and boning the fish. Speed was essential and it has been estimated that the very best girls could gut at the rate of 20,000 fish per day! Great dexterity ensured that they ended the season with little or no damage to their hands. [Real photographic postcard from the 1930s by the photographer Violet Banks A.R.P.S., and a Gaelic series, black and white printed *Cairt Phostail circa* 1897. A contemporary photograph of this scene, made from the original negative, is in the Cathcart Collection held by the National Museums of Scotland under reference 1735]

7. A truly atmospheric scene from the 1930s when *"If herring-drifters be not racing in from the fishing grounds so as to be in time for the auctioning....of their catches....they are moving out from the pier to various curing stations, whose agents have purchased their respective catches."* [Real photographic postcard by Valentine's of Dundee]

8. *"We find ourselves in a street with houses on one side and a dirty shore on the other. It is neither quaint nor beautiful, but pathetically ordinary. The several shops consist of post office, a 'sweetie shop' and several stores. One could not truthfully describe the stores as grocer shops, when their contents include oilskins, gully knives, newspapers and miscellaneous articles of men's, women's and children's wear."* (**'To Introduce the Hebrides' Iain F. Anderson, 1933).** The pack ponies have gone and the motor car has arrived, though in the early 1930s it was still outnumbered by the onlookers! *"The first motor car was imported into the island in 1926 - a mixed blessing,"* reported John Lorne Campbell in **'The Book of Barra'** (1936), and the car in this picture, with the 1929 Paisley registration XS 2246, may well have been one of the first. Beware, today a one-way traffic system now operates down the street. [Real photographic postcard by the *Scholastic Souvenir Company* of Blackpool, *circa* 1933]

21

9. Photographed some 60 years ago but little has changed in the street. A Mr. W. Bruce had his name over the door of the shop in the small lean-to on the right, but a doctor's surgery has recently been erected on this spot. A B.P. petrol pump stands in the street as a monument to the motor-cars that *"...have invaded the islands now,"* wrote Walter Mursell in **'Isles of Sunset'** (1931), *"but they are as yet unspoiled places, with occasional visitors but no trippers."* [Real photographic postcard by Valentine's of Dundee, mid 1930s]

A messenger in Barra. (Copyright.)

Pack-Ponies, in Outer Hebrides. (Copyright.)

10 - 12. Three images in Castlebay towards the close of the last century, but these hardy little animals are seldom seen in the island today. *"....it is no unusual occurrence to find as many as twenty or thirty horses....and ponies....moving hither and thither across this great sandy stretch (Traigh Mhor) at one time. And in the heat of the noonday sun they appear afar off like a tribe of nomads trekking with their impedimenta across an Eastern desert."* (**Summer Days among the Western Isles'** Alasdair Alpin MacGregor, 1929). [Gaelic series, black and white printed *Cairt Phostail circa* 1900. A contemporary photograph of *'Pack Ponies in Outer Hebrides'*, made from the original negative, is in the Cathcart Collection held by the National Museums of Scotland under reference 1730 and is inscribed *'At Castlebay, July 1897']*

An am Bagh-a-Chaisteal. (Copyright.)

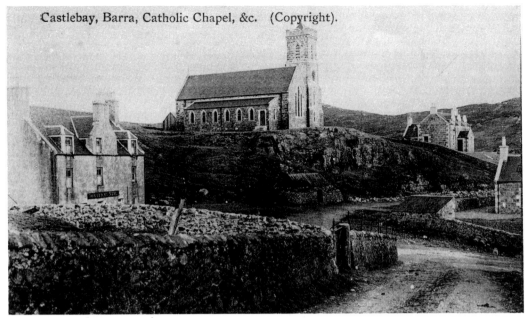

Castlebay, Barra, Catholic Chapel, &c. (Copyright).

13. The imposing church of Our Lady, Star of the Sea, dominates the sky-line of Castlebay. *"Surrounding the bay are some half-dozen good and well-placed buildings, the Roman Catholic Church....and a few neat slate-roofed houses belonging to successful tradesmen...."* The Catholic church at Craigston was the only one in Barra until the priest, Father (later Canon) Chisholm, undertook the task of erecting this building, *"....beautiful in design, the workmanship is substantial enough to withstand the Hebridean gales for a century or two to come,"* he wrote later, *"....It will be a landmark for the daring fishermen of Barra, as they venture to and from their deep-sea excursions...."* (**'The Catholic Highlands of Scotland'**, Dom. Odo Blundell O.S.B., 1917). The church itself was consecrated just over a century ago in 1889. [A Gaelic series, black and white printed *Cairt Phostail circa* 1902, photo *circa* 1895]

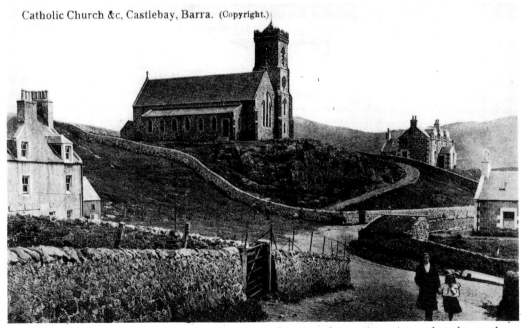

Catholic Church &c, Castlebay, Barra. (Copyright.)

14. Taken just a year or two later from the identical spot as the previous picture, but changes have already taken place. Donald MacNeil, owner of the large building on the left, has added a small shed to the side of his store in the Square; the black-house has been demolished and a boundary wall built around the church. [A Gaelic series, black and white printed *Cairt Phostail circa* 1903, photo *circa* 1897]

24

A Creel Pony, Castlebay, Barra. (Copyright)

15 & 16. At the top of the main street in the Square stands the grand store of Donald MacNeil the local *'General Merchant'*. A picture taken a few years earlier shows a Creel Pony outside the premises; today the modern motorized equivalent uses this exact spot alongside the *new* Castlebay Hall. [A Gaelic series, black and white printed *Cairt Phostail circa* 1900, and an anonymous, black and white printed card of the store, *circa* 1910]

The Hotel, Castlebay, Barra

17. Castlebay Hotel and bar - previously leased from the Cluny estates by local man Jonathan McLean, who owned many of the grazing islands to the south of Barra - was in the ownership of Allan MacLeod when this photograph was taken. It is still a MacLeod family enterprise today, although Allan might be surprised by the extensions added by his grandson George. The road as seen here was no match for the traffic of the late 1900s and, like the hotel, has been enlarged over the years. Trade was undoubtedly good in 1948 when Joan Greenwood, Basil Rathbone, Gordon Jackson, James Robertson-Justice, and about eighty other people, spent some 3 months in Barra during the making of that enjoyable Compton Mackenzie/Ealing Classic film, *'Whisky Galore!'* [A sepia printed postcard by Raphael Tuck, published for the 'Sole Agent', Hugh Mac-Donald of Oban, late 1930s]

HOTEL COUPONS

As erroneous impressions have been held by many of the travelling public regarding the cost of hotel living in the Highlands and Islands of Scotland, David MacBrayne, Ltd., have arranged with the principal Hotels throughout the districts served by their Royal Route Fleet to accept Coupons at reasonable rates for accommodation and meals. Full particulars regarding these Coupons, with List of Hotels accepting same, can be had free on application.

Complete List of Lodgings, Boarding-Houses, and Hotels in the Western Highlands and Islands of Scotland can also be had free on application to

DAVID MACBRAYNE, Ltd.,
119 Hope Street, Glasgow.

Caledonian MacBrayne have now discontinued their *Hotel Coupons* scheme, so please do not trouble them with your enquiry! This advertisement appeared in the 1912 issue of their 'Summer Tours in the Western Highlands and Islands of Scotland" book, lavishly illustrated throughout its 184 pages and priced at just 3d. [Bob Charnley Collection]

18. Said to be Patrick Sinclair of Kentangaval, originally from Berneray (Barra Head), the **Barra Giant** is seen here outside the Castlebay Inn with some of his smaller friends! He is a good 6 inches taller than the door opening, and whilst estimates of his height vary wildly the consensus of opinion is that he was about three inches under 7 feet tall. [Black and white printed card, with undivided back, published anonymously *circa* 1901]

Castle Bay, Barra

19. This Victorian panorama was photographed from above the township of **Nask** - *Nasg* - in the latter years of the nineteenth century, with the loch and bay, and the island of Muldoanich. Once a thriving deer-forest, the isle provided venison for the table of the MacNeil and served as a place of banishment for potential troublemakers. How different is the scene from this viewpoint today! [A hand-coloured, printed card by Valentine's of Dundee, published *circa* 1912 from a photograph taken during the period 1875 - 85]

Kentangval. (Copyright.)

20 & 21. Two glimpses of **Kentangaval** - *Ceann Tangabhal*, an important Victorian township on the west side of the island about a mile from Castlebay itself. *"On leaving Castle Bay all signs of prosperity are at an end, not even in South Uist are the houses more wretched or the scraps of cultivated ground more pitiable."* [G-F] An early 20th century diary in the author's collection has this entry, brief though it be: *"About a mile from Castlebay town there is an interesting village or collection of pure crofters huts which we visited."* A comment made by a tourist upon seeing this hamlet, whilst spending three hours in Barra on his return voyage from St. Kilda during the month of August 1913. [Gaelic series, black and white printed *Cairt Phostail circa* 1902]

Kentangval. (Copyright.)

Lochmor us Dun Mhicleoid.
(Copyright.)

22. Loch Mor agus Dun Mhicleoid. *"Turning westward from Castle Bay one comes suddenly....upon a little castle, a very toy in fortifications, standing upon a little island in a little lake..."* An ancient ruin of a tower or keep near Tangusdale, it is also known as Castle St. Clair and features in Elizabeth Helme's Victorian novel 'St. Clair of the Isles'. Close by this spot is yet another of those ubiquitous island wells, this particular one being dedicated to St. Columba. [A Gaelic series, black and white printed *Cairt Phostail circa* 1902]

Crofters Stock-Taking in Barra

23. The announcement in the House of Commons was straight forward - Her Majesty's Government intended to set up a Royal Commission to *"inquire into the conditions of the crofters and cottars in the Highlands and Islands of Scotland."* In less than ten weeks, on Saturday 26 May 1883, the members of the Napier Commission were in Barra taking evidence from interested parties. Three years later, in June 1886, the Crofters Act became law, and although it was not a cure-all it did provide crofters with security of tenure and the right to a fair rent. The site of these Victorian crofts is close to the Hebridean Perfume building just before Halaman Bay. [A printed black and white postcard produced *circa* 1904 from an original photograph of the mid 1880s by the George Washington Wilson Studio]

24. Halaman Bay, and photographer Violet Banks has captured the grandeur of the area, though the five people in her picture are lost in the expanse of sand. *"No one with a musical ear and an atom of poetry in his spiritual make-up would be loth to linger here, either in winter or summer, when the western tide is pouring in through the creeks and caverns and among the fallen rocks of Halaman Bay...."* (**Summer Days among the Western Isles').** Close to this spot, in 1974, the Isle of Barra Hotel was built. [Real photographic postcard from a photo by Violet Banks, A.R.P.S., taken in the 1930s]

CARRYING PEAT IN CREALS
ISLE OF BARRA

E 832

25. *"On a warm summer day,"* wrote Alasdair Alpin MacGregor in his evocatively over-romantic, 1929 book, **'Summer Days among the Western Isles'**, *"I have counted as many as fifty ponies employed at the creeling of the peats in the Dark Glen of Barra, and in carting them to Greian, Cliat, Cuier, Allasdale, Bruernish, Balnabadach, and the several other crofting townships scattered throughout the Isle of Barra....On scanning the hillsides one sometimes is amazed to notice, perhaps a mile away, a couple of ponies with peat-filled creels being led by a small barefooted boy down the face of rocks on which the average town-dweller would feel positively squeamish."* [Real photographic postcard by the *Scholastic Souvenir Company* of Blackpool, *circa* 1930]

26. For anyone unfamiliar with the island of Barra, the overwhelming majority of its people adhere to the Church of Rome. This fact is mentioned here for the good reason that no early postcard of the Church of Scotland building in Barra has been unearthed so far, but the ponies are a fitting introduction to the Reverend Archibald McDonald, minister of that kirk from 1871 to 1932. *"He was a familiar figure in Barra, of which he seemed to form an integral part. His kindly, indolent personality became an institution in the island. His pony also became infected with the same indolent spirit and never pulled her gig beyond walking pace. In fact, the pace of the minister's pony was accepted in Barra as the "superlative" of slow motion."* (Donald Buchanan **'Reflections of the Isle of Barra'**). [Real photographic postcard from a photo by Violet Banks, A.R.P.S., taken in the 1930s]

27. The old inn at **Northbay** - *Bagh A Tuath*. Could this unassuming little building be the *"ruinous rendezvous"* that Father McKenzie, the parish priest at Craigston from 1893 (and then later at Northbay), believed it to be? According to one contemporary writer the licensed premises was a blemish on the fair isle and a thorn in the flesh of the pastor, and he would visit it regularly, not hesitating *"to use his heavy cane upon those whose recreation he rudely interrupted."* Clerical zeal these days is tempered with a little more understanding and less physical violence! [Real photographic postcard by the *Scholastic Souvenir Company* of Blackpool, *circa* 1928]

28. On the **Traigh Mhor**, and Barra's unusual landing-strip. Famed throughout most of the world as the runway that is washed twice daily by the tide, the cockle strand has served Northern & Scottish Airways, British European Airways and Loganair, since 1935. A modern terminal building was opened in 1978, replacing the little shed which once stood on the opposite side of the road and acted as airport booking-office and radio shack. [A printed, black and white postcard published by Davidson & Son in their "Ideal Series"]

The Meccano Magazine for March 1959 showing the 'Air Ambulance on the Beach at Barra'. Two of the illustrated articles in this issue were "Scotland's Air Ambulance Service' and 'David MacBrayne and his Steamers'. [Bob Charnley Collection]

29. Eoligarry - *Eolaigearraidh,* with the island of Fuday in the background and the late eighteenth century edifice, Eoligarry House, at the bend in the road. *"Time was when, in the walled garden laid out at Eoligarry by the old MacNeils of Barra, great quantities of fruit were grown. Today the garden at Eoligarry is a pathetic wilderness of grasses and weeds, and of trees and shrubs that winter winds and storms have stunted and seared."* (A.A. MacGregor **'Summer Days among the Western Isles'**). [Unattributed, photographic postcard]

30. The view seen by the traveller approaching Northbay from the west, with the road from Eoligarry coming in at the left, joining the continuous circular road back to Castlebay. Visually little has changed, although a statue dedicated to St. Finnbarr, the patron saint of Barra, has been erected on the little island in the centre of this bay, and commercial buildings now intrude on the rock-strewn sky-line. [Real photographic postcard by the *Scholastic Souvenir Company* of Blackpool, *circa* 1926]

31. Resist the temptation to re-visit the old inn at Northbay *(illustration 27)* - situated less than a quarter of a mile away - and continue along the east side of the island towards **Northbay Catholic Church.** Built in 1906, it was here that Father McKenzie administered to the spiritual needs of that *"generation of magnificent and handsome young men"* of Bruernish, who had been saved from the sinful pleasures of their former haunt. A lifelong friend of Father Allan MacDonald of Eriskay (of whom more later), Father William McKenzie was yet one more *"devoted and industrious priest"* whose life was shortened by his considerable work-load and total unselfishness. He died just before the outbreak of World War I. [Black and white printed postcard published by unidentified 'W.D.T. & S' *circa* 1908]

32. The old school at Northbay, redundant as a seat of learning but now a family home and comfortable guest-house. The addition of railings on either side of this road gives a greater feeling of security as one drives across the narrow causeway today. [Real photographic postcard by the *Scholastic Souvenir Company* of Blackpool, *circa* 1930]

33. A glimpse of a cottage in **Brevig** - *Breibhig. "The people (of Barra) are generally a cheerful race - very different from the saddened dwellers in the bogs of South Uist, though their homes are much the same, with only one hole in the thatch to admit light, and emit smoke. The fire burns in a hollow in the middle of the floor, and round it gather all the picturesque details of such an interior - the cattle on one side, human beings on the other; the big black pot, the heaps of fishing-nets, or tarry wool, and the blue peat smoke veiling all."* (**'In the Hebrides'**, Mrs. C.F. Gordon Cumming, 1883). The 20th century brought an end to such conditions, and when this picture was taken the interior of the home was warm, cosy and clean, the beasts having been moved to other accommodation elsewhere on the croft. [Real photographic postcard by the *Scholastic Souvenir Company* of Blackpool, *circa* 1933]

Castlebay from Heaval.

34. Always a sight to lift heart and soul, however many times one sees it; the southern isles as seen from Heaval, at 1260 feet the highest point in Barra. Beyond Castlebay lie the islands of Vatersay - with the large horse-shoe bay - Sandray, Pabbay, Mingulay and Berneray, where sits the Barra Head lighthouse. [Real photographic postcard from a photo by Violet Banks, A.R.P.S., 1930s]

35. The island of **Vatersay** - *Bhatarsaigh* - deserves more than a passing mention because of its recent history. Farmed for most of the last century, the island was owned by Lady Gordon Cathcart when it came to public attention in the first decade of this century. Briefly, with too little land and too many families living around Castlebay, Nask and Kentangaval, the people turned their eyes towards Vatersay. Officialdom was slow to react to their pleas for extra acreage and Lady Cathcart was unyielding. Some movement did take place and sixty acres were leased for the growing of potatoes, but the crop failed and the people were thwarted with every subsequent legal move and request they made. But on a summer day in 1906, the affair came to a head when a Castlebay man crossed to Vatersay just after sunrise, built a hut, thatched it, and lit a fire in the hearth before the sun had set. Thus, under an ancient law of Scotland, he became the possessor of the land. Others followed him, arrests were made and prison sentences meted out, but the eventual outcome was that a Government body, the Congested Districts Board, purchased the island from Lady Cathcart, and provided holdings for crofter-fishermen from Barra. A causeway, opened in 1991, now links the two islands. [An anonymous, sepia printed postcard from the mid 1930s]

36. This view of the **East bay of Vatersay** shows the stern half *"of a fairly large vessel that, while on a voyage to Northern Russia, was torpedoed during the Great War. I was told by a man in Castlebay,"* wrote Alasdair Alpin MacGregor in 1929, *"that eight or ten puffer-loads of timber were taken off that part now aground and rusting in Vatersay Bay, and covered with barnacles."* Sadly, Vatersay has been a grave-yard for many ships over the centuries, and a monument erected above *Traigh Siar* on the west side of the island commemorates one of the greatest tragedies; the loss of the sailing ship *Annie Jane* in September 1853. **'Shipwrecked on Vatersay!'** (Maclean Press, 1992) reveals the true story behind this disaster. [Real photographic postcard by the *Scholastic Souvenir Company* of Blackpool, *circa* 1932]

Vatersay, Barra

SAND DUNES, VATERSAY, ISLE OF BARRA.

E.5186

Royal Mail Steamer "Plover" leaving Castlebay, Barra

37. For our journey to South Uist we take David MacBrayne's steamer *'Plover'*, built in 1904 specifically for the Island service. An admirable vessel, she was not however without one critic, that much-travelled writer A. A. MacGregor again: *"A boat infinitely superior to the Cygnet or the Plover is required for the Barra route. No one who has travelled to Castlebay with a south-west wind blowing and the full might of the Atlantic sweeping toward Coll and Tiree would hesitate in urging the dire necessity for placing a swifter, stronger and steadier boat on the Barra route."* On a July day in 1918 the *'Plover'* encountered a U-boat between Tiree and Barra, and when firing began some of the crew and passengers took to three lifeboats. Accusations of drunkenness apart, the passengers and crew would have been fearful for their lives; only three years earlier a U-boat had sunk the *'Lusitania'* off Ireland with the loss of nearly 1200 lives. On board the *'Plover'* a gallant crew-member returned fire with the ship's gun; the submarine fled and the vessel continued her voyage to Barra. Fortunately no lives were lost and one of the lifeboats headed the right way; it arrived in Castlebay the following day. A sound case for a fare refund! [Sepia printed postcard published by Francis Frith of Reigate *circa* 1920]

ERISKAY
Eiriosgaigh

"An island of South Uist parish, Outer Hebrides, Inverness-shire, separated by a channel 2 miles wide from the S end of South Uist island. It is notable for having been the place where Prince Charles Edward first set foot on the kingdom of his ancestors, 23 July 1745. The channel between Eriskay and South Uist is used as a boat harbour for the export of local produce. There are a post office, a public school and a Roman Catholic Church. Population 454." *(Extract (part) from Volume II, 'Ordnance Gazetteer of Scotland: A Survey of Scottish Topography, Statistical, Biographical and Historical.' New Edition c. 1895).*

Dun, Staak-a-Bhreabadair, Sound of Barra. (Copyright.)

38. Dun, **Stac-a'-Bhreabadair,** in the Sound of Barra, better known as Weavers Castle on Stack Island off Eriskay. *"We stayed in Barra for the night, and next day resumed our voyage....to Eriskay, a fact which I mention only for the sake of recalling our sight of the Stack Islands' wave-worn rocks now only occupied by sheep. One - Creag Mhor, the big rock, romantically crowned with a ruined tower - is the subject of weird legend and is indeed suggestive to the imagination. Nothing more absolutely solitary could be imagined, and the utter loneliness of the position is accentuated by the extreme minuteness of the island, which seems as if the rush of the surrounding sea might any moment dash it to pieces."* [G-F] [A Gaelic series, black and white printed *Cairt Phostail circa* 1902]

39

In Bala, Eriskay, where Prince Charlie slept first night in Britain. (Copyright.)

39. A view of **Bala** - *Baile* - where, according to the caption, Prince Charlie slept his first night in Britain. *" 'Is not this Prince Charlie's house?' we ask of a man who stands in the doorway. He laughs at the form of our question. "It's mine now, in any case," he answers, hospitably standing aside that we may enter. It is just like a score more within a stone's throw, and has probably changed little in a century and a half."* [G-F] In a note to the Preface of her 1902 book Miss Goodrich-Freer regretted the recent loss of Prince Charlie's cottage, demolished with the permission of Lady Gordon Cathcart, the absentee owner of the island. [A Gaelic series, black and white printed *Cairt Phostail circa* 1902]

40. Eriskay Post Office photographed in the very early years of the twentieth century. *"There is a school-house and a post-office and a church and a shop - at least sometimes there is a shop or, rather, sometimes there are some things in the shop."* [G-F] In 1885 a remarkable man, Dougal MacMillan, became the first postmaster in Eriskay, or more correctly sub-postmaster as the office was a sub post office. Ada Goodrich-Freer met him personally during her visit to the island in the 1890s but she probably did not have enough of the 'second-sight' to anticipate the longevity of the man; Dougal was still in the same employment at the time of his death in 1945. [A Gaelic series, black and white printed *Cairt Phostail circa* 1902, photo *circa* 1902]

41. An t-Urramach Maighistir Ailean agus am Pobull, an deidh an aifrionn, an Eiriosgaigh. Sunday Mass is over and the people satisfy the demands of the photographer whilst their parish priest, Father Allan MacDonald *("...a stately figure of a man in his soutane and beretta...")*, approaches a small group of people standing apart from the rest, their isolation and mode of dress suggesting they are visitors to the island. This beautiful little church opened in 1903, just two years before Fr. Allan's untimely death at the early age of 46 years. *"For priest and people,"* states the writer of his obituary, *"life in the Hebrides is made up of hardships and trials which dwellers on the mainland little know or understand."* Maighistir Ailean *("I wouldn't know who they were talking about if they called me "Father MacDonald!" ")*, a native of Lochaber, died after a short illness, *"and his funeral was such as could be seen nowhere else. Immediately after the coffin walked the clergy, followed by the women and children, children on foot and children in arms, mothers and their families weeping and praying for the fond father who was making his last journey to his home in their midst; the aged too, men and women all took their part in that last act of veneration to one they loved so well."* And on that October day in 1905 the people of Eriskay made a remarkable gesture at the grave-side. As the men stepped forward, preparing to fill in the grave, they were moved away by the mourners, *"who sobbing, laid soil and sods gently with their hands over the coffin, and so the grave was filled and covered."* (**'The Catholic Highlands of Scotland'**, Dom. Odo Blundell O.S.B., 1917). [A Gaelic series, black and white printed *Cairt Phostail circa* 1904]

The Post Office, Eriskay, Outer Hebrides. (Copyright.)

An t-Urramach Maighistir Ailean 'us am Pobull,
an deidh n' aifrionn, an Eriskay. (Copyright.)

PUBLIC SCHOOL, ERISKAY, SOUTH UIST.

E.1413.

42. The **Public School** in the late 1920s. Not unexpectedly Father Allan devoted much of his time overseeing the education of the Eriskay children; he had been Chairman of the School Board of South Uist in 1889, and was responsible for the appointment of a non-Gaelic speaking Englishman, Frederick G. Rea, to the post of head teacher of Garrynamonie school, the first Catholic to hold that post, in the predominately Catholic island, since the Reformation. [Real photographic postcard by the *Scholastic Souvenir Company* of Blackpool, *circa* 1928. Collection of Cailean Maclean]

43. Eriskay harbour as it looked in the 1880s, the thatch of the black-houses rather than fishing-boats stealing the scene. But one ship, known the world over because of the film *'Whisky Galore!'*, is especially associated with the island. The S.S. *'Politician'*, an 8,000-ton cargo vessel, sailed from Liverpool in February 1941 with over 250,000 bottles of the very finest whisky. For the hazardous voyage across the North Atlantic to Jamaica and New Orleans, a route via the Minch was imposed by the Admiralty on the captain, a decision which sealed the fate of that treasure store of whisky. Bad weather and unfamiliar waters contributed to the disaster, but in reality the captain and crew were lost and ended up aground on a rock-strewn sandbank, less than a mile from this harbour. The rest is history and is fully recorded in Roger Hutchinson's 1990 book **'Polly'.** [Hand tinted postcard by Valentine's of Dundee *circa* 1920, produced from a photograph of the 1880s]

44. *"...Her head a little bent, and on her mouth, a doubtful smile dwelt like a clouded moon in a still water."* (Tennyson) It is a personal thought, and the passing of time cannot change the actuality, but one hopes that this little *'Maid of Eriskay'*, as photographer Violet Banks called her, had a happy childhood on her remote island. Not too many children appear *alone* on a picture postcard; she was surely proud of that! [Real photographic postcard by Violet Banks A.R.P.S., *circa* 1933]

Eriskay Harbour, South Uist

BRINGING HOME THE PEATS-ERISKAY, S.UIST

45. The late Twenties, but this picture shows the important status of the pony to an island community and particularly in connection with the gathering of the peat. *"Let us consider for a moment,"* wrote Alasdair Alpin MacGregor in his 1925 book **'Behold The Hebrides!',** *"how the Isleswoman toils each year at the peat-moss, in order that an ample store of fuel may be laid in for the cold, wet winter with its long, dark nights....The carrying of the peats is done almost entirely by women and children, who trail all day long with laden creels between the peat-moss and the spot where other members of the family are busily engaged in stack-making. You must bear in mind that the peats have to be attended to in all weathers; and the days which have been assigned to them are seldom spent otherwise, unless torrential rains, which are anything but uncommon in these regions, have made the peat-moss inaccessible, or impossible to work."* [Real photographic postcard published anonymously in the period 1928 - 33, but bearing a date code as used by Valentine's of Dundee]

SOUTH UIST
Uibhist a Deas

"An island and a parish of the Outer Hebrides, Inverness-shire. The climate, for a Hebridean one, is far from being moist, and the air is generally mild and pure. The uplands are devoted chiefly to the rearing of black cattle, to the improvement of which by the introduction of new breeds, great attention has for some time been paid. Cheviot sheep have been introduced with some advantage. South Uist has regular steamer communication with Glasgow, Oban, Dunvegan, Portree, and Loch Maddy, and has a post and telegraph office, under Lochboisdale Pier, at Howmore. One Roman Catholic chapel is at Ardkenneth, was built in 1829 and contains 400 sittings. Another in Benbecula was built in 1884; a third is in Eriskay; a fourth is at Bornish; and a fifth is at Dalibrog, was built in 1868, and contains 500 sittings. There are nine public schools with total accommodation for 1024 children. Population 5821 of whom 5532 were Gaelic-speaking." *(Extract (part) from Volume VI, 'Ordnance Gazetteer of Scotland: A Survey of Scottish Topography, Statistical, Biographical and Historical.' New Edition c. 1895).*

LOCHBOISDALE, SOUTH UIST.

46. The pier at **Lochboisdale** - *Loch Baghasdail* - with the famed Lochboisdale Hotel to the right. The white-painted edifice in the centre was, until recently, a shop of West Highland Farmers & Crofters; currently it stands empty, only the Post Office remains in a small corner of this once thriving building. [Printed postcard by Valentine's of Dundee with date code for 1927; from a photograph *circa* 1890]

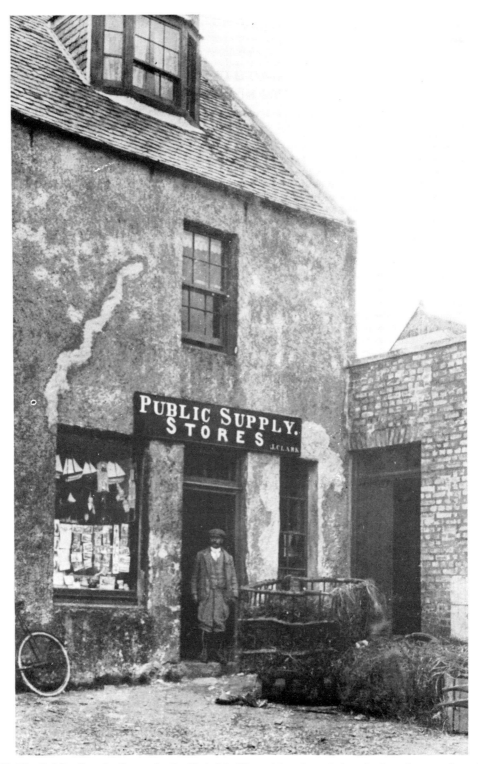

47. The **Public Supply Stores** by Lochboisdale Pier, with a fine window-display of postcards and toy yachts presumably designed to entice the Edwardian tourist rather than the local shopper! Standing by the door is Johnny Clark, a beloved figure in Lochboisdale and owner of the shop at this time. [Unattributed, black and white printed postcard *circa* 1910]

A small card *circa* 1910, produced for John Clark and advertising the home spun Tweeds, available from his General Supply Stores by Lochboisdale Pier. [Cailean Maclean Collection]

48. The scene looking inland from the pier. *"There is, thank Heaven, but one South Uist in the world, though in poverty, misery, and neglect, the island of Barra, sixteen miles south, runs it very close."* [G-F] The large building in the centre of the picture is now the local branch of the Royal Bank of Scotland, attached to the house of the incumbent manager. [A Gaelic series, black and white printed *Cairt Phostail circa* 1903, photo *circa* 1898]

49. The S.S. *'Hebrides'* at Lochboisdale pier. *"Come into South Uist on a calm summer evening filled with mystic lights on sea and loch and hill, and you will think yourself in a land of enchantment, wherein elves or fairies might be seen at any moment; come into it on a day of storm and cloud when the hills are swathed in mist, and the sea is laced with foam, and driving rain is making holes in the lochs like small shot, and you will think you have come to the haunts of the gnomes or even the Sons of Thunder."* (**'Isles of Sunset'** Walter Mursell). [A sepia printed postcard *circa* 1922 with imprint 'D. Ferguson & Co., Lochboisdale']

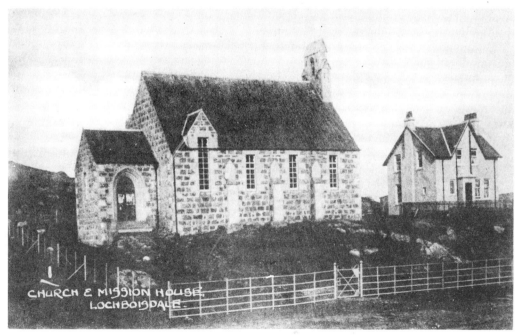

50. The Church & Mission House at Lochboisdale, built specifically for the incomers involved with the herring trade many years ago; neither building serves the spiritual needs of the people today. The Mission House has already taken on the appearance of a fine secular establishment but the old church remains unused. Only in the fullness of time will we see what becomes of it, but rumours are plentiful! [Sepia printed postcard with imprint 'Clark Series, Lochboisdale', *circa* 1920]

GLASGOW
AND
WEST HIGHLANDS.

CIRCULAR TOURS
(About 7 Sailing Days),
to the
OUTER ISLANDS
by the

Splendidly fitted
Steamer,
Lighted by
Electricity.

"HEBRIDES"

Superior
Accommodation,
Bathroom,
&c.

EVERY TEN DAYS
From GLASGOW at 11 a.m.
and
GREENOCK at 4.30 p.m.
on arrival of Train from (Caledonian, Central Station) Glasgow.

*Cabin for the Round, Board Included, £9.
CRUISES to ST. KILDA and LOCH ROAG on Special Dates.
*Cabin for Round, Board Included, £10.

For Dates of Sailings and Berths apply to

JOHN M'CALLUM & CO.,

PARTNERS { H. YOUNG.
W. YOUNG.

87 UNION STREET,

Telegraphic Address:
" M'Callum, Glasgow."

GLASGOW.

Phone:
2193 Central.

*Berths in Four-Berthed Rooms 2/6 extra, in Two-Berthed Rooms and Deck Cabins,
5/- extra; and Passengers remitting by own cheque (London excepted), will please
include cost of exchange.
The Tour occupies about Seven Days, but any meals supplied beyond Eight
Days for Tourists will be charged at the rate of 9/- per day.

The front cover of McCallum's leaflet for tours aboard the S.S. *Hebrides, circa* 1919-20. [Bob Charnley Collection]

Lochboisdale. (Copyright.)

51 & 52. *"South Uist is surely the most forsaken spot on God's earth."* [G-F] Two photographs of **Loch-boisdale,** taken 30 years apart, looking towards the harbour and the pier. Miss Goodrich-Freer, regrettably, was not impressed by what she saw in South Uist in the 1890s. *"The very existence of the island of South Uist is itself a tragedy which shames our civilization,"* she added, but her anger was aimed directly at the owner of the island and not the destitute islanders. Compare the scene today; the white-washed house looks just the same but nearby, in this line of buildings, the 'Sea Breeze' tea-room provides hot food for the present generation of hungry travellers whilst the old kelpers hut, visible on the right of the 1928 picture, has completely disappeared. [A Gaelic series, black and white printed *Cairt Phostail circa* 1903, photo *circa* 1898; and a real photographic postcard by the *Scholastic Souvenir Company* of Blackpool, *circa* 1928]

LOCHBOISDALE

Lochboisdale Hotel, South Uist, by Oban.
Simon Mackenzie, Proprietor.

53. Queen Victoria was sovereign, the Empire was strong, and the **Lochboisdale Hotel** was being successfully managed by Simon Mackenzie, who became the proprietor in 1892. It was, and still is, a favourite venue for anglers familiar with the waters of Bharp and Lower Kildonan. A fire destroyed part of the hotel in 1918 but it was rebuilt within a year or two, albeit on a smaller scale. It is a great comfort to know that a warm, cosy room awaits you when the ferry from Oban is running late, and you arrive at Lochboisdale long after darkness has fallen and the mists have rolled in. A blessed car journey of just 100 yards from pier to hotel is all that is required! [A Gaelic series, black and white printed *Cairt Phostail circa* 1903, photo *circa* 1897]

An advertisement for the Lochboisdale Hotel from the 1935 issue of MacBrayne's Highlands and Islands time-table. "You can dine in London one night and in Lochboisdale the next," is the confident boast! [Bob Charnley Collection]

Lochboisdale, "Marconi" pole.

54. An Italian in his twenties, yet this pole in a remote corner of the kingdom carried his name in the earliest years of the century. *"Signor Marconi has the sublime confidence of genius,"* announced the New York correspondent of the *'Daily Telegraph'* on December 16 1901, *"that the signals he received at St. John's, Newfoundland, last Wednesday and Thursday, were from the wireless telegraph station at the Lizard, Cornwall."* This mast was erected on high ground at the rear of the post-office some years after the Telegraph man had added to his report: *"Marconi considers that he has surmounted the difficulties in regard to transoceanic wireless telegraphy, and that it is now a real live factor in the industrial and commercial life of the world."* [A Gaelic series, black and white printed *Cairt Phostail circa* 1904]

Bute Hospital, Dalibrog, South Uist. (Copyright.)

55. *"One gleam of brightness there is, a cottage hospital, built and maintained by the Marchioness of Bute, on whom, needless to say, the island has no claim whatsoever."* [G-F] Built in 1894 and situated at Daliburgh - Dalabrog, it was run by *"...three devoted women, constantly fighting such disease as comes of starvation, bad water, no drainage, and the accidents inseparable from sea-faring life in open boats on a dangerous coast."* Miss Goodrich-Freer also permits us to glimpse inside the newly-opened building where she finds that *"everything is done to show consideration for the feelings of the people, as for example in having all the rooms on one floor, for a staircase has all the terror of the unknown..."* She also commented on the good garden of mixed vegetables and flowers, and the after-care which encouraged the women to sew and the children to learn by *"gentle example and quiet self-restraint."* One hopes that the hospital can survive its current problem and celebrate a well-deserved centenary, serving the needs of the local community. [A Gaelic series, black and white printed *Cairt Phostail circa* 1901, photo *circa* 1897]

56. Eaglais Chaitleacach agus Tigh an t-Sagairt, Dalabrog. Commanding the heights with splendid views to the south, the Catholic Church and presbytery of St. Peter's at Daliburgh. Ada Goodrich-Freer had the good fortune to meet two of the priests who lived here in the 1890s; Father Allan MacDonald and Father George Rigg. Both subsequently gave their lives for the people of Eriskay and South Uist. Fr. Allan arrived in 1884 but his great energy became diminished by bad health and he moved to Eriskay. Fr. George, his successor at Daliburgh, died in 1897 of typhoid fever, contracted whilst caring for a family stricken with the ailment. Dedicated is an inadequate word with which to describe these men; they were undoubtedly saintly souls, but I personally regret that there is no written reference to either pastor, or a memorial to their lives, within the walls of this fine church. [A Gaelic series, black and white printed *Cairt Phostail circa* 1901, photo *circa* 1896]

53

Eaglais Chaitliceach 'us Tigh an t-Sagairt, Dhalibrog. (Copyright.)

Copyright
SU7

South Lochboisdale, South Uist

57. South Lochboisdale and the house and one-time store of local merchant Donald Ferguson. *"It (lies) in a well-sheltered nook beside an arm of the sea,"* wrote teacher F.G. Rea in his diary for 1889. *"A large roomy comfortable-looking stone house, with slated roof, was attached to a sort of general store. In front of the house was the first attempt at a garden I had seen since landing; and, wonder of wonders - trees!"* (**'A School in South Uist'** F.G. Rea, edited by John Lorne Campbell, 1964). [A sepia printed postcard by Raphael Tuck, published for the 'Sole Agent', Hugh MacDonald of Oban, late 1930s]

58. Treabhadh an Uibhist-a-deas; a crofter, somewhere in South Uist, guides his plough behind the pair of horses whilst a cleric, hat in hand, stands and watches. [A Gaelic series, black and white printed *Cairt Phostail circa* 1902]

59. The inn at **Pollachar** - *Pol A Charra* - was once a Change-House; a place where one could wait for the ferry when travelling between Eoligarry in Barra and South Uist. Eventually it provided food and drink, and has served the island voyager for close on 200 years. It apparently dates from the mid eighteenth century and, rumour has it, was almost complete in 1746 when Prince Charles Edward Stuart was wandering through the land, just a few miles away. The low barn on the left is now roofless and derelict, and a bar has been tacked onto the front of it, extending the line of the original buildings which outwardly remain unchanged. From the car park one can enjoy fine views across to Barra and glimpse the distant Dun on Stack Island *(illustration 38)*. [An anonymous, black and white printed postcard *circa* 1912]

A Kelp Maker's Hut, South Uist

60. Fish apart, the sea also provides great quantities of seaweed, useful on any island as a cheap source of manure for the field. But burning the weed, or kelp, also produces a commodity used in the production of glass and soap, and from the mid 1700s for a period of some seventy years or so, the price of Hebridean kelp soared to unbelievable levels. As it required 24 tons of seaweed to produce a single ton of the alkaline ash it was especially labour intensive, and as a consequence the population of South Uist increased considerably between 1800 and 1830. With production costs of about £5 a ton and a sale price of over £20, the product generated huge profits for the landowner, Macdonald of Clanranald, but little for the people of Uist, many of whom were required to cut and burn the kelp as part of their tenancy contract. By the late 1820s new methods of producing alkali had reduced the profits for Macdonald and his fellow landowners, and mounting debts forced many of them to sell off most of their lands. [Hand coloured, printed postcard by Valentine's of Dundee *circa* 1918, photo *circa* 1885]

Prince Charlie's Cave, South Uist

Reg: G. MacDonald of Clanranald Esq.
Bo.t of Browne, Miller & McLeith

1809					
Apr. 4	To 1 Hh.d of Choice 1st Growth Claret Wine of Vintage 1802 in Wood	£105	..	..	
1810					
Aug.t 7	1 Hh.d Choice 1st Growth Claret Wine "Vin pur" 1802 in Wood	105	..	..	
	1 Hh.d Choice 1st Growth Claret Wine of Kirwan Cantanac	105	..	..	
	2 Hh.ds of 1st Growth Claret Wine of Mariton La Fitte 1802	210	..	..	
	1 Pipe of Choice old London particular Madeira Wine	145	..	..	
	Charges on these Wines				
	124 doz Quart Bottles for these 2/8	16	10	8	
	64 doz English Pint Bottles 2/6	8	..	..	
	16 Gross of Corks for D.o 10/6	8	8	..	
	Wax for D.o	..	16	6	
	Cooperage Fining Corking Claret 4/ ea.	1	..	..	
	D.o " " Madeira	..	10	6	
	Porterage Bottling Claret 5/ ea.	1	5	..	
	D.o " Madeira	..	8	..	
	4 doz: Choice red Burgundy 168/	33	12	..	
	2 1/2 doz: Vin daix Champaign 168/	21	..	..	
	6 doz Choice white Hermitage 126/	37	16	..	
		801	6	8	
	By three months interest of discount	10	6	8	
		£791			

Settled the above as J. Hampton
Receipt   Browne, Miller & Co.

On paper watermarked 'J.Whatman 1810', the Georgian wine bill of **Macdonald of Clanranald**. Supplied by Messrs. Browne, Miller & Co. of Leith, it includes five hogsheads (52.5 Imperial Gallons per hogshead) of various 1802 Clarets, a Pipe (105 gallons) of Madeira Wine, together with 124 dozen empty quart bottles, corks and wax. A few dozen 'Choice red Burgundy', 'White Hermitage' and two and a half dozen 'Champaign' suggests that 1810 was a good year for Hebridean kelp. The total of £791 spent by Clanranald on his drink, between April 1809 and August 1810, would be the equivalent of £20,000 today. [Bob Charnley Collection]

61. The military disaster of Culloden and the offer of a £30,000 reward (*£1 million* in today's terms), brought about the futile wanderings of Prince Charles Edward Stuart within these Hebridean isles. Spurred on by the bounty his pursuers pressed the Prince relentlessly, forcing him and his band to move frequently between Benbecula, Harris, Lewis, the Uists and Skye. A cave on the east side of the island, in a small bay between Lochs Skipport and Eynort, was yet one of his many alleged hiding places between April and June 1746. [Hand coloured, printed postcard by Valentine's of Dundee *circa* 1918, photo *circa* 1885]

62. The Post Office, Howmore - *Tobha Mor*, in the late 1890s. With such a neat building it is appropriate to read a contemporary comment that *"Much labour is spent over the thatch of the houses, which, if attended to from time to time, may last for forty years."* [G-F] In 1843 the postal authorities established a receiving-house at Howmore, served initially by runners but later (1880s) by a carrier on horseback, whose weekly salary was £1 and included an allowance for the horse! [A Gaelic series, black and white printed *Cairt Phostail circa* 1901, photo *circa* 1897]

GROGARY, SOUTH UIST.

63. Grogarry Lodge, owned by South Uist Estates, is today available for private rent and provides a commodious base for groups of people with similar interests, including bird-watching, shooting and fishing. [Printed 'Bromotype' postcard by Valentine's of Dundee with the date code for 1927]

Pier, Lochskipport, South Uist. (Copyright.)

64. Loch Skipport - *Loch Sgioport* - pier was one of the few good things that Lady Gordon Cathcart, the owner of the island, provided. Built in 1879, cynics might suggest that she intended it be used for removing the islanders not shipping in food and livestock. Whilst this is a peaceful spot, there is a certain sadness about the place today. Passenger ships no longer arrive from Glasgow, the walls are in a bad state of repair and the pier supports rise from the sea like the fingers of a drowning man. On a summer evening you could find yourself totally alone here, sharing the landscape with a herd of itinerant ponies. [A Gaelic series, black and white printed *Cairt Phostail circa* 1901. photo *circa* 1898]

Lochskipport, South Uist. (Copyright.)

65. Four years older than the pier at Loch Skipport, the S.S. *'Dunara Castle'* sailed these seas for over seventy years, her final voyage being in 1948. This remarkable 450-ton vessel sailed from Glasgow with cargo for many of the western isles, and during the summer months extended her route to visit remote St. Kilda, giving her passengers a few hours ashore. *"We then went South to a lovely little place called Skipport. Here we stayed some one and a half hours unshipping and shipping goods. A school of porpoises were play-*

ing in the loch, and from the top of the hill on which I stood in the sunlight the loch looked perfect, with a large number of gulls about and quite a number of porpoises. There is a good road to the pier from the country, and a special breed of goat here also, a kind they say like the mountain goat. We saw two or three crofters' houses, or rather huts. The people here all talk Gaelic and apparently no English. We left this beautiful spot by its narrow entrance in the evening." (Extract from a 1913 diary - Bob Charnley Collection) [A Gaelic series, black and white printed *Cairt Phostail circa* 1901, photo *circa* 1898]

Scottish Home-Industries.
President:
Her Grace the Duchess of Sutherland.

Manchester Exhibition,
St. James' Hall,
13 & 14 October, 1903, at 2 p.m
Presidents:
The Lord Mayor and the Lady
Mayoress of Manchester.

Boys Fishing, Uist.

66. 'Boys Fishing, Uist.' A postcard issued by the Scottish Home Industries Association to advertise their attendance at the Manchester Exhibition, held in St. James' Hall, Manchester, 13-14 October, 1903. A *Cairt Phostail* of the same photograph, with the caption *'Iasgairachd'*, was already on sale in South Uist at this time. (illustrationI) [An anonymous, black and white printed postcard of 1903, original photo taken *circa* 1900. A contemporary photograph of this scene, made from the original negative, is in the Cathcart Collection held by the National Museums of Scotland under reference 1691]

South Ford and Benbecula from Carnan. (Copyright.)

67. At the **South Ford,** the crossing point for our journey northward to the island of Benbecula. *"....it is at eventide that you ought to visit the Fords, if you are at all imaginative....And if you should tarry until darkness has fallen around you, and the sands are aglow with the soft half-light of the Aurora Borealis and of the many quivering stars, you will become conscious of the meaning of those boulders that by the hand of man have been placed at intervals to guide in safety across the Fords the pilgrim, who may be mist-enwrapped or night-encircled....you will hear the lonely cry of the sea-birds....at the line of the ebbing tide.... and your ears will be attuned to the sea-music that the breakers of the limitless Atlantic have been making on these Hebridean sands for a million years and more; and you will find yourself at one with the Infinite."* (**'Behold the Hebrides!'** Alasdair Alpin MacGregor, 1925). In 1943 this ford was bridged, an important war-time link for the people of Benbecula with the port at Lochboisdale. [A Gaelic series, black and white printed *Cairt Phostail circa* 1902, photo *circa* 1898]

BENBECULA
Beinn na Faoghla

"An island of South Uist parish, Outer Hebrides, Inverness-shire. It lies between the islands of North and South Uist, being separated from the former by a sound 3.5 miles broad, containing a number of small islands and islets, from the latter by a channel half a mile broad in the narrowest part and dry at low water. Though little better than a patch of wilderness, half swamped in ocean, Benbecula was an ancient property of the chiefs of Clanranald, had once a nunnery, and still has remains of an old baronial castle. Much land, since about the year 1830, has been reclaimed from a state of moss and great attention is given to the raising of live stock and fishing. A missionary of the royal bounty has a church on the island, where also is a Roman Catholic church (1884; 400 sittings). Mrs. Gordon's Female Industrial School, with accommodation for 218 children, has an average attendance of about 80. Population 1659." *(Extract (part) from Volume I, 'Ordnance Gazetteer of Scotland: A Survey of Scottish Topography, Statistical, Biographical and Historical.' New Edition c. 1895).*

CREAGORRY, BENBECULA.

68. The road through Creagorry hamlet - *Creag Ghoraidh,* on the wind-swept island of Benbecula, the highest point being Rueval at just 408 feet. The present Post Office stands very close to the site of the old one, on the right of this picture, with the greatly enlarged hotel on the left. [An anonymous, black and white printed postcard *circa* 1925]

Creagorry, and hills of South Uist. (Copyright.)

69 & 70. Two views of the 1885 inn at Creagorry, with the sign over the door proclaiming Archibald Maclean to be the licensee. In the distance South Uist, now joined with Benbecula by the causeway which, technically at least, ended the right of either place to call itself an island, though the visitor would be very unwise to echo this opinion! [Two Gaelic series, black and white printed *Cairt Phostail circa* 1902]

Creagorry Hotel, Benbecula. (A. MacLean, Proprietor)

The Post Office, Benbecula

71 & 72. This building had served as the island police station for a number of years but in the late 1870s it was turned over to the postal authorities and became **Creagorry Post Office,** Benbecula's second, the first having been established at Nunton in the 1840s. [An anonymous, sepia printed card showing the original frontage, and a Gaelic series, black and white printed *Cairt Phostail circa* 1904, photo 1903. A contemporary photograph of this scene, made from the original negative, is in the Cathcart Collection held by the National Museums of Scotland under reference 1729, and bears the date '*10 August 1903*']

Benbecula. (Copyright.)

73. A croft in Liniclete - *Lionacleit*. The remains of similar buildings are scattered either side of the road running through this township, but the Dark Island Hotel and *Sgoil Lionacleit* represent the architectural influence of twentieth century-man on the landscape. [A photographic card by Violet Banks A.R.P.S. *circa* 1935]

Copyright. BNBA. 7. The Manse and Church of Scotland, Benbecula. Raphael Tuck & Sons Ltd London.

74. The Church of Scotland kirk and Manse, close by the War Memorial and on the road through Church Hill and Griminish. The date-stone above the porch is inscribed "A.D. 1886". Three churches once lined the same side of this road; between here and St. Mary's *(illustration 76)* stands the building of the old United Free Church, now converted into self-contained flats. [A sepia printed postcard by Raphael Tuck, postally used in 1938]

The Lodge, Benbecula

75. Across the road from the Church of Scotland stood Sorrell House - now a doctor's surgery - overlooking Loch Olavat. The story goes that at the beginning of the century the owner of this property, a drapery merchant from Ireland, disappointed with the quality of his land, imported large quantities of Irish soil to enrich the ground in the garden. The nature of his business also kept him away from home for long periods, but on his return his faithful wife ran a flag up the flag-pole to signal his return to the neighbours! [A sepia printed postcard by Raphael Tuck, published for the 'Sole Agent', Hugh MacDonald of Oban, late 1930s]

76. Beinn-na-faoghla, Eaglais Cnoc-Mhorra, agus Tigh-chleir. *"I have grateful recollections of pleasant entertainment, both in manse and presbytery, in this island of Benbecula...."* [G-F] The Catholic Church of St. Mary was opened in August 1884, some six years after the presbytery. A contemporary account of the opening ceremony relates how the Bishop, with fellow clergy and guests, arrived at Lochskipport on board a large steam yacht chartered by a Mr. Campbell of Lochnell. After an overnight rest they, and a large crowd of people from South Uist, set off on a 16 mile journey in a downpour of rain, arriving at the new church at 1 p.m. A great Pontifical Mass was sung and the *"Islanders were rejoiced beyond description at seeing ceremonies which had been unknown in the island for centuries."* And such was their enthusiasm that day, *"...they followed his Lordship and the visitors for a long way on their return journey."* (**'The Catholic Highlands of Scotland',** Dom. Odo Blundell O.S.B., 1917). [A Gaelic series, black and white printed *Cairt Phostail circa* 1902, photo *circa* 1897]

77. 'Each Chleibh'. The ever-faithful, omnipresent pack horse. [A Gaelic series, black and white printed *Cairt Phostail circa* 1902]

PETERS PORT & PIER, BENBECULA, SOUTH UIST.

78. Peter's Port and Pier completed in 1896 and something of a white elephant even in those days. The sea entrance was not particularly good but the land approach was even worse - there was no road! It was all an utter waste of time and public money, but such things are not uncommon today; motorways with bridge supports on the hard-shoulder, and by-passes which require by-passing within a generation. Ah! the benefits of hindsight. [Real photographic postcard by the *Scholastic Souvenir Company* of Blackpool, *circa* 1932]

Cille-Chalumcille, Benbecula. (Copyright.)

79. Cille-Chalumcille, the ruins of the chapel of St. Columba. Erected on an ancient site, it dates back some 1500 years but today the setting is somewhat incongruous, being so close to an airfield and a military camp. [A Gaelic series, black and white printed *Cairt Phostail circa* 1902, photo *circa* 1898]

80. This image, though not a postcard, may bring back fond memories for some despite the passage of time. The back of this private photograph tells us all we need to know with one exception. *Who was Kate?* The men were all members of the **R.A.F. Station Police** in Benbecula on 5 May 1944, and on the back row, from left to right, are Cpls. Jamieson, Billen, Fairbanks, Crook, Harvey and Morrison, who signed the picture for *'Kate with Best Wishes and Happy Memories.'* In the front row, left to right, are Cpls. Austin and Brooke, with Sgts. Shimmins and Murdoch, and Cpl. Kennedy. R.A.F. Benbecula became operational in June 1942 within 15 Group, Coastal Command. It provided aircraft for convoy escort, anti-submarine duty, search and rescue and general reconnaissance with Hudson, Flying Fortress, Wellington and Swordfish. [Private photograph]

BENBECULA WELCOME, ROYAL VISIT

81. Many Royal persons have visited the islands over the years, the current trend being to try and slip in and out quietly (not easy with secretaries, protection officers and a camera crew). On this occasion in September 1960, the islanders turned out to welcome Her Majesty, the Queen Mother, who arrived *publicly* to open the North Ford causeway between Gramsdale and Carinish via the island of Grimsay. And so the islands were joined, allowing an unbroken journey of around 75 miles from North Uist down to the Eriskay ferry at Ludag. [Real photographic card, lacking details of the publisher but with a date code as used by Valentines]

NORTH UIST & BERNERAY
Uibhist a Tuath & Eilean Bhearnaraigh

"An island and parish of the Outer Hebrides, Inverness-shire. The island is bounded on the W and NW by the Atlantic Ocean, on the NE by the Sound of Harris, on the E by the Little Minch, on the S, separating it from Benbecula, by a narrow, complicated, shallow strait, densely packed with isles and islets and partly fordable between low water and half tide. Looked at from almost every vantage ground it seems to defy description or exploration, so intricate and broken is the outline. The whole of the territory thus cut into fragments is a dreary, flat, marshy moorland. The inhabitants have shared very largely in the miseries so common throughout the Hebrides and the Highland shores of the mainland. It contains the post-office stations of Lochmaddy and Carinish. Population 4187 of whom 3927 were Gaelic-speaking. Bernera, an island and a quoad sacra parish in Harris parish, Inverness-shire. The island lies in the Sound of Harris, about 1 mile N of the nearest part of North Uist and 5 miles SSW of the nearest part of Harris. It has a post office under Lochmaddy, the church is a Government one and was built in 1829. Population 501. '(Extracts (part) from Volume I and VI, "Ordnance Gazetteer of Scotland: A Survey of Scottish Topography, Statistical, Biographical and Historical.' New Edition c. 1895).

H. M. Mails on North Ford. (Copyright.)

82. H.M. Mails on North Ford. The great advantage of the modern causeway is clearly obvious upon seeing this postcard. Moving the mail between Benbecula, Grimsay and North Uist, was accomplished in many ways between 1802 and 1960, the horse being just one method. Rowing-boat, pony and cart or tractor and trailer, the old adage was that *'the mail must get through',* and thanks to generations of MacDonalds it usually did. [A Gaelic series, black and white printed *Cairt Phostail circa* 1902, photo *circa* 1897]

An Tigh-Osda, Carinish. (Copyright.)

83. An Tigh-Osda, with a fine view of the old inn at Carinish, on your left as you approach from the south. Bartholomew's, Edwardian 'Tourists and Cyclists' map (Sheet 18, Uist & Barra), pinpoints the various inns, temperance or otherwise, scattered around the main crossing routes between the islands. Some are now just ruins but local tales and legends testify as to their importance for the wet and weary traveller! *"....we are soon at the North Ford, It is about sunset, as that is usually a convenient time for crossing, and this ford, being considerably wider than the other, is the one especially to be considered....by dint of putting our feet and possessions on to the seat of the carriage, we advanced for a mile or so, and then we had to wait for an hour before it was safe to proceed....All around us were the waters of the Atlantic ocean which, not far off, was raging and hurling itself with its wonted might, but here silently ebbing and clearing a pathway for us mere human things whom a single wave could destroy...."* [G-F]. [A Gaelic series, black and white printed *Cairt Phostail circa* 1902, photo *circa* 1897]

Teampull na Trionaid, Carinish. (Copyright.)

84. Teampull na Trionaid, the combined ruins of two small chapels, known separately as MacVicar's Temple and Trinity Temple, the latter dating from the earliest years of the 13th century. The MacVicars were considered to be fine teachers, instructing the sons of the Chiefs in their understanding of the English and Latin languages. [A Gaelic series, black and white printed *Cairt Phostail circa* 1902, photo *circa* 1900]

85. Carinish by Lochmaddy, at this time the store of local merchant Donald Maclean. Today it is a private house but it continues to be known by the name carved into the stone over the lower left-hand window, *'Temple View'*, a reference to its uninterrupted outlook towards *Teampull na Trionaid*. [An anonymous, black and white printed postcard *circa* 1915]

86. Clachan, Locheport. A busy 20th century road junction; ahead is the A 865 to Bayhead, Hougharry and the coastal route via Sollas to Lochmaddy; whilst to the right, the direct road to Locheport and Lochmaddy. [A Gaelic series, black and white printed *Cairt Phostail circa* 1902, photo *circa* 1897]

Loch Eport, North Uist

87. The Kelpers pier at Locheport where *"the kelp trade is kept alive at the chemical works, the tangle weed being collected largely at Loch Boisdale in South Uist. The total quantity of kelp manufactured in a recent year (the largest, however, for several preceding years) was about 200 tons, which was shipped to Bowling on the Clyde."* **(Ordnance Gazetteer of Scotland,** Volume VI, *circa* 1895). [Hand coloured, printed postcard by Valentine's of Dundee *circa* 1918, photo *circa* 1890]

88 & 89. At **Locheport** - *Loch Euphoirt. "We left Dunvegan at about 2 o'clock and crossed the Minch to Locheport in North Uist. Here we were pleasantly surprised; the entrance was a very narrow one with two mountains on the right entrance and one on the left not far off. The rocky coast was grand and I should say that the Captain of the "Hebrides" must have been a careful navigator to take a boat, even of the size of ours, through such a channel. After going some distance the land is very much lower and the loch is fairly populated on the south side for these isles. The farms, or small holdings, do not show any signs of harvest. We were soon surrounded by boats again. The ferry or inland cargo boat was a much larger one than usual and took in a large quantity of stores, apparently taking a long time to take them on board. This boat goes all over the inland part and distributes what it has on board to the inhabitants. We also met a number of boats containing women selling home-made Harris Tweed. It looked very good and several passengers bought some for 3/3d per yard."* (Private diary entry, made by a passenger aboard the S.S. *'Hebrides'* in 1913, during a trip from Glasgow to St. Kilda - Bob Charnley Collection). [Real Photographic postcards in the "McCallum, Orme & Co., Ltd.'s, Series *circa* 1928]

Loch Eport Ferryboat

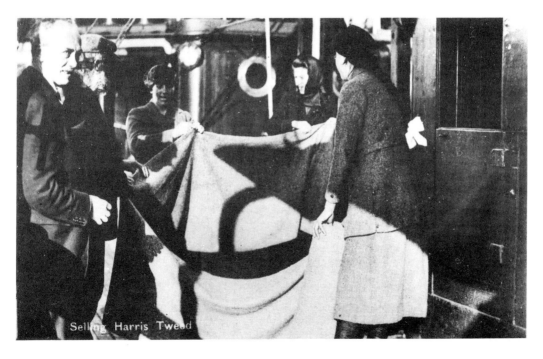

Selling Harris Tweed

Langash Lodge. (Copyright.)

90. At **Langass** - *Langais* - some 6 miles from Lochmaddy, this private hunting lodge had been built for the use of guests of the owner of the island, but times and needs have changed and today it is a six-bedroomed hotel, overlooking Loch Langass close by Locheport. [A Gaelic series, black and white printed *Cairt Phostail circa* 1902, photo *circa* 1897]

Barp, Langass. (Copyright.)

91. Barp, Langass, a large chambered cairn, vaguely dated by various authorities as having been erected between the years 3000 BC and 1000 BC. Thought to be the burial place of an unknown hero of a distant age, it is at least 70 feet in diameter with a height exceeding 16 feet. [A Gaelic series, black and white printed *Cairt Phostail circa* 1902, photo *circa* 1897]

Westford Inn, by Lochmaddy.

92. The forbidding exterior of the **Westford Inn,** at Clachan Kirkibost - *Cladach Chirceboist,* photographed after the licence had been transferred from the Tighary Inn in 1896 and passed to Mrs. Macaulay, whose name appears on the sign over the door. *"A conspicuous square house,"* as Erskine Beveridge described it in his 1911 book **'North Uist'**, *"originally built for a doctor's residence. It now bears the name West Ford Inn."* A local constable stands nearby - surely not trouble?, but the windows are very un-Hebridean and were removed from Kilmory Castle in Argyll-shire, one time residence of Sir John Campbell Orde, proprietor of North Uist until his death in 1897. [A Gaelic series, black and white printed *Cairt Phostail circa* 1902, photo *circa* 1897]

Creag Hastin, North Uist. (Copyright.)

93. Creag Hastin. *"A group of curious rocks upon the top of a hillock, with the appearance - from a distance - of the ruins of an old castle."* Reputed to be the home of *sithichean* (fairies), this outcrop, set in the district of Paible, acted as a pulpit for travelling preachers in the mid 1800s. [A Gaelic series, black and white printed *Cairt Phostail circa* 1902, photo *circa* 1897]

Fishing with a "Tabh" net in Outer Hebrides. (Copyright.)

94. Fishing with a 'Tabh' net, best described by one familiar with its construction, Erskine Beveridge, as being *"wrought from the roots of the grass Carex Flacca...one inch mesh, conical shape, four feet in length by a width of 19 inches across its mouth, thence tapering to a point at the other end."* [A Gaelic series, black and white printed *Cairt Phostail circa* 1902, photo *circa* 1897]

76

Parish Church of North Uist. (Copyright.)

95. The **Parish Church of North Uist,** not, as might be supposed, in the main centre in Lochmaddy, but at Balranald - *Baile Raghaille.* A beautiful little building, it replaced the old church at Kilmuir then in a state of disrepair, and could hold some 400 parishioners. North Uist born, Donald MacDonald, *"a tall man, loosely built with the ascetic-look of a saint...."*, became parish minister when the church was opened in 1892. *Maighistir Domhnull,* as he was known, was considered an excellent Gaelic preacher, *"delivering his message in a quiet, orderly and persuasive manner."* (**'Hebridean Heritage'** Rev. Angus MacVicar, 1966). [A Gaelic series, black and white printed *Cairt Phostail circa* 1902, photo *circa* 1897]

Hougarry. (Copyright.)

96. The crofting township of Houghgarry - *Hogha Gearraidh.* In *some* respects it was a lucky place to be living in during the first half of the 19th century; it did not suffer the same fate as many other North Uist townships and was not cleared of its people. *"The farther one recedes from the seaports, from the large farms of the wealthy tacksmen, from the domains of the shopkeeper and the schoolmaster, the brighter do the souls of the cottars grow, the opener their hands, the purer their morals, and the happier their homes."* ('The Hebrid Isles' R. Buchanan, 1883). [A Gaelic series, black and white printed *Cairt Phostail circa* 1902, photo *circa* 1897]

Making tea on a Uist fair. (Copyright.)

97. Making tea on a Uist fair and a young girl hangs on to her best hat whilst the older woman attends to the fire and kettle. Visit a fair or the North Uist Agricultural Society's Annual Show at Hosta today and the tea and hot-dogs may very well be provided by members of Her Majesty's Armed Forces; a positive bonus on a wet and windy day on the machair! [A Gaelic series, black and white printed *Cairt Phostail circa* 1902, photo *circa* 1897]

98. Prize-giving at the **North Uist Cattle Show** in the late 1930s. The committee for the present N.U. Agricultural Society present a most praiseworthy Show for the residents of Berneray and North Uist, with a magnificent array of trophies and small cash prizes. But what a test for the various judges! Over 45 classes of cattle, sheep and poultry; more than 35 classes for kitchen garden produce and flowers, and nearly 100 other classes in different sections. The 'Heaviest Cabbage' class however should pose no problems for one adjudicator! [Real photographic postcard from a photo by A. Manson, postally used from Sollas in 1938. Collection of Domhnall MacCormaig]

78

99. Mary Matheson of Malaclete - *Malacleit,* photographed in Glenelg, Inverness-shire, in 1889, along with her husband John MacLeod (centre) and three of their children. Mary was born in Malaclete in 1847, the second child of cottar Donald (son of John, son of Donald) and Ann (MacAskill). Her uncle, Neil Matheson, married Mary MacDougall, one time governess at Balranald to the factor's daughter Jessie MacDonald. Jessie's influence with her father helped Neil to obtain a site for a shop in Balranald, whilst Mary Matheson's father received a croft at 11/1 Malaclete. Mary's younger sister Kirsty married a Finlay Morrison who was born on the island of Pabbay, but when the island was cleared his family moved to Harris. Most of their children went to Port na Long, Skye, but one daughter, Ann, married John MacDonald and their grandson is currently a driver with the Harris buses. Whilst pursuing this genealogical theme (courtesy of Bill Lawson, *Co Leis Thu?* Northton, Harris), mention should be made of Mary's only brother, Donald *(Domhnall Ban).* His daughter Marion married Donald Stewart of Middlequarter, and gave birth to William, whose widow and daughter live there still. Marion's sister, Kate, married Lachlan MacDonald of 1, Malaclete (formerly Baleshare), and descendants abound! All that (and much more!) from an anonymous photograph in an anonymous album, discovered in a second-hand bookshop in Stockport, England, and now the subject of the book **'The Summer of "89'** (Maclean Press, 1991). [Postcard published in 1990 by Firtree Publishing of Fort William, (' "Bob Charnley Collection'), from the original sepia photograph of 1889]

SELLAS AIRCRAFT, NORTH UIST

G-ACSM

E5285

100. Northern & Scottish Airways of Glasgow was formed in 1934, flying from Glasgow to the isles and including Skye and Barra within its schedule. Sollas - *Solas* - was the chosen landing site in North Uist, but failure to secure the Royal Mail contract led to the demise of the airline, formed by Captain David Barclay and George Nicholson, and it amalgamated with Highland Airways the following year, emerging as Scottish Airways Ltd. This photograph was taken in 1936 and is a rare little gem for any collector of old postcards. [Real photographic postcard by the *Scholastic Souvenir Company* of Blackpool; posted from Lochmaddy in 1937]

Newton Ferry. (Copyright.)

101. The Post and Telegraph Office at **Newton Ferry** - *Port Nan Long.* Established in the late 1870s, this building stood at the end of a four mile long, dead-end road but provided a vital postal link with the island of Berneray in the Sound of Harris. From a different site at Newton Jetty, a small car ferry now carries the mail to Berneray in under 10 minutes, whilst foot passengers may travel to Leverburgh in Harris in about 45 minutes, a useful alternative to the Cal-Mac ferry from Lochmaddy to Tarbert. [A Gaelic series, black and white printed *Cairt Phostail circa* 1902, photo *circa* 1897]

In Berneray of Harris. (Copyright.)

102 - 104. Three views of sites in the small island of **Berneray** in the Sound of Harris. A mere thumbprint of an island in a current road atlas of Scotland (the only named location being 'Borve'), one can only stand and watch in amazement at the procession of Dutch, French and German-registered cars boarding the tiny ferry at Newton. The American visitors, until they speak, are less obvious in their Glasgow-registered hire cars! The whole world now knows the secret; this is the island to visit! [Two Gaelic series, black and white printed *Cairt Phostail circa* 1904, photos 1904. A contemporary photograph of the *'In Berneray of Harris'* postcard (Rishgarry Quay), taken from the original negative, is in the Cathcart Collection held by the National Museums of Scotland under reference 1708, and is dated *'17 July 1904'*. The Broad Bay view is a real photographic postcard by the *Scholastic Souvenir Company* of Blackpool, *circa* 1930]

Cladh Maelrubha, Berneray, Harris. (Copyright).

BROAD BAY, BERNERA, LOCH MADDY.

Sheep Clipping in Outer Hebrides. (Copyright.)

105. A group of crofters somewhere in the Outer Hebrides. The exact location is unimportant, sheep provide a useful income for many throughout the Long Island. Before the familiar Orb-mark can be applied to Harris Tweed it must be shown than the wool has been *"Spun, dyed and finished in the Outer Hebrides and handwoven by the Islanders in their own homes in the Islands of Lewis, Harris, Uist, Barra and their several purtenances and all known as the Outer Hebrides."* The wool itself, however, must be pure virgin wool produced in Scotland, and the clip from Hebridean sheep is considered more suitable for carpets than jackets or skirts, and is usually shipped directly to the mainland! Now out of print, though it still turns up in second-hand bookshops, Francis Thompson's **'Harris Tweed The Story of a Hebridean Industry'** (1969) is recommended reading. [A Gaelic series, black and white printed *Cairt Phostail circa* 1903, photo *circa* 1900]

Genuine Harris Tweed

We have set our seal "The Ram" as a passport to you and your customer that the cloth is the Real Article.

YOU HAVE OUR GUARANTEE THAT THIS IS SO.

We attach to every length the name of the weaver by whom it has been woven and every three yards bears the registered trade mark of The Harris Tweed Association Ltd.

Buying Harris Tweed from this magnificent Bunch you have the fullest confidence that the garment you supply is exactly as described.

28/28½ inches wide, 11 ozs to the yard, single width.

Price 10/3 per yard.

Every number always stocked by:-

James Hare Ltd., Leeds & London.

DISTRIBUTORS OF GENUINE HOME MADE HARRIS TWEED.

A 1930s shop leaflet for Harris Tweed. [Bob Charnley Collection]

106. Blashaval - *Blathaisbhal* - from **Strumore** - *Struth Mor;* the view as seen from the small causeway on the A 865, a few hundred yards from its junction with the road to Lochmaddy Pier. [Real photographic postcard by the *Scholastic Souvenir Company* of Blackpool, postally used in 1935]

Feill a Loch-na-madaidh.

107. Feill Loch nam Madadh at the turn of the century, with cattle and horse dealers inspecting, haggling and striking bargains. [A Gaelic series, black and white printed *Cairt Phostail circa* 1902, photo *circa* 1897. A contemporary photograph of this scene, made from the original negative, is in the Cathcart Collection held by the National Museums of Scotland under reference 1700]

A Uist Market. (II. Copyright.)

A Uist Market. (I. Copyright.)

108 - 112. A selection of views taken at some of the regular Fairs or Markets in the Uists and Benbecula. A wonderful opportunity for the ladies to get together, and perhaps buy a small trinket or household item from a stall-holder. The men, meanwhile, indulged in the buying and selling of animals, with just the odd drink to quench their thirst. *"Naturally, there was a liberal consumption of "the barley bree" at the market, but, the consumers being all hardened vessels, no one appeared any the worse, nor even any the livelier - and liveliness is by no means a characteristic of these gentle quiet folk, most of whom seem to be naturally of a somewhat melancholy temperament."* (**'In the Hebrides',** Mrs. C.F. Gordon Cumming, 1883). [All Gaelic series, black and white printed *Cairt Phostail circa* 1902, photos *circa* 1897]

Feill a' Loch-na-madaidh. Copyright.

Air feill an Uidhist. (Copyright.)

Toys and Sweets at a Uist fair. (Copyright.)

113. A general view of part of Lochmaddy, the principal town of North Uist and former *"rendezvous of pirates"* (**Privy Council Register of 1616,** Vol. X, page 634). Amenities include a seasonal Tourist Office and Youth Hostel; the estate-owned Lochmaddy Hotel, a handful of shops, a bank, a post-office, and several comfortable guest houses. The all-important Lochmaddy Pier provides the traveller with a link to the island of Harris (for Lewis), and to Skye (for the mainland). [A Gaelic series, black and white printed *Cairt Phostail circa* 1902, photo *circa* 1897]

Buain corc, an Loch-an-madaidh. Copyright.

114. Buain corc, an Loch nam Madadh; cutting the corn at Lochmaddy. Approaching Lochmaddy from the direction of Sollas or Carinish, take the first road to the left towards the Lochmaddy Hospital; this photograph was taken just a few yards along the track, the buildings on the horizon being the old Post Office, the present Court and the old Court-House. [A Gaelic series, black and white printed *Cairt Phostail circa* 1902, photo *circa* 1897]

Lochmaddy, School. (Copyright.)

115. The charm and apparent peace of the Victorian school in **Lochmaddy**. The school buildings are on the left, the rest belonged to the teacher! [A Gaelic series, black and white printed *Cairt Phostail circa* 1902, photo *circa* 1897]

Sponish House. (Copyright.)

116. Sponish House, once a splendid Victorian mansion and home for the Sheriff, is now a stark ruin (after a recent disastrous fire), whilst the area around the building is the site of an alginate factory opened in the 1950s, processing seaweed for various commercial purposes including use in food products and beauty care preparations. [A Gaelic series, black and white printed *Cairt Phostail circa* 1902, photo *circa* 1897]

Lochmaddy. (Copyright.)

117. Lochmaddy under a blanket of snow. Continuing along the road shown in *illustration 114,* one eventually arrives at this spot, the administrative centre of Lochmaddy as it looked in the late 1890s. The prominent building in the centre of the picture is the County Court Building with the walled garden of the old Court-House to the right. [A Gaelic series, black and white printed *Cairt Phostail circa* 1902, photo *circa* 1897]

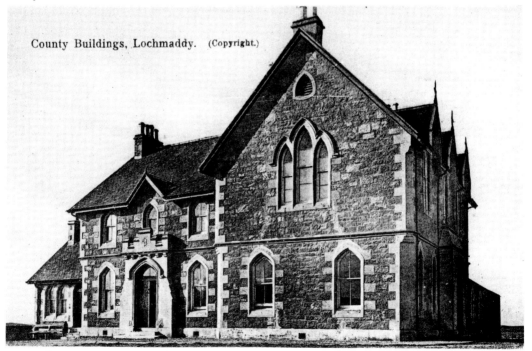

County Buildings, Lochmaddy. (Copyright.)

118. County Buildings, Lochmaddy, and from the rooms within this fine building the administration of North Uist was accomplished and justice dispensed. The sheer size and quality of this - and some other edifices in the area - indicates the importance of Lochmaddy and reflects on the numerous officials and sporting visitors who worked and played here. [A Gaelic series, black and white printed *Cairt Phostail circa* 1902, photo *circa* 1897]

119. Ofic am Phuist an Loch nam Madadh. Just across the road from the County Buildings stood the Lochmaddy Post Office in the early years of the century. Until 1885 a black-house had been used for the sorting of the mail, but although this larger property was close to the administration buildings it was considered to be too far from the pier and was itself closed down in 1905. [A Gaelic series, black and white printed *Cairt Phostail circa* 1903, photo *circa* 1903]

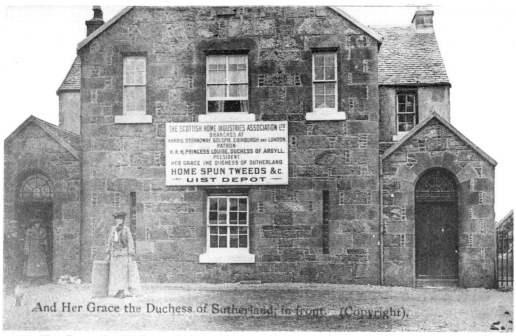

And Her Grace the Duchess of Sutherland, in front. (Copyright).

120. Her Grace the Duchess of Sutherland outside the North Uist branch of the Home Industries Association at Lochmaddy. Opened in 1900 and equipped with modern looms provided by the President, the Duchess herself, great quantities of Harris Tweed were produced here, but now, alas, no more. This building, once the old Court-House for the island, is a private guest-house with a fine walled garden. Dwell here awhile, and on a warm summer evening one just might hear the sound of the bagpipes drifting along on the breeze. [A Gaelic series, black and white printed *Cairt Phostail circa* 1902, photo *circa* 1901]

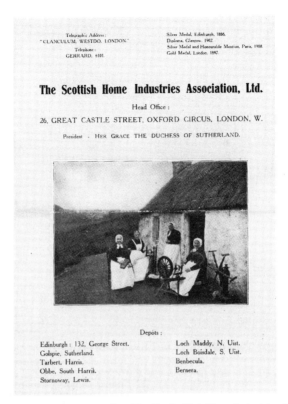

Telegraphic Address :
"CLANCULUM, WESTDO, LONDON."
Telephone :
GERRARD, 6101.

Silver Medal, Edinburgh, 1886.
Diploma, Glasgow. 1902.
Silver Medal and Honourable Mention, Paris, 1900.
Gold Medal, London. 1897.

The Scottish Home Industries Association, Ltd.

Head Office :

26, GREAT CASTLE STREET, OXFORD CIRCUS, LONDON, W.

President - HER GRACE THE DUCHESS OF SUTHERLAND.

Depôts :

Edinburgh : 132, George Street.	Loch Maddy, N. Uist.
Golspie, Sutherland.	Loch Boisdale, S. Uist.
Tarbert, Harris.	Benbecula.
Obbe, South Harris.	Bernera.
Stornoway, Lewis.	

The cover of a four page Edwardian catalogue produced by the Scottish Home Industries Association. Harris and St. Kilda Tweed was 5/- a yard and a 'top of the range' Spinning Wheel cost 2 guineas. [Bob Charnley Collection]

121. Sean Laimhrig agus buth Iain Dhomhnullaich an Loch nam Madadh. [A Gaelic series, black and white printed *Cairt Phostail circa* 1902, photo *circa* 1897]

122. Sean Laimhrig agus Tigh-na-Cuirte etc. Loch nam Madadh. *"In Loch Maddy there are pianos, and drawing-rooms, and afternoon tea, and people call upon one, and leave cards, and take photographs, and read newspapers and are kind and friendly, and a wholesome reminder of some of the duties and pleasures of normal life."* [G-F] In this panoramic view the County Building dominates and the quay *(illustration 121)* is now seen in relation to its surroundings. [A Gaelic series, black and white printed *Cairt Phostail circa* 1902, photo *circa* 1899]

123. The Bank of Scotland at Lochmaddy, a most solid Victorian building which is still standing but offers physical comfort now rather than financial advice; it is the *'Old Bank House'* guest house. Banks, being very cost-conscious with our money these days, tend to be slightly more modest affairs now. [A Gaelic series, black and white printed *Cairt Phostail circa* 1902, photo *circa* 1900]

The Store, Lochmaddy, North Uist

Our only shop. J. Mᶜ.G.

124. The Store in Lochmaddy with the brief, hand-written message, *"Our only shop"*. In the early years of the century it stood in splendid isolation, but now the cars and heavy lorries using Cal-Mac's *'Hebridean Isles'* pass within yards of the building, conveniently situated at the junction of the road from the ferry terminal and that to the Court and police station. It is gaunt and empty today, its windows boarded against the ravages of the unkindly weather and inquisitive eyes. [Anonymous, black and white printed postcard *circa* 1908]

Temperance Hotel, Lochmaddy

125. A Temperance Hotel in the early years of the century, this establishment now serves the needs of the traveller seeking souvenirs, not looking for a bed for the night. It is more recognisable if one searches for it by name rather than by using this old picture which was taken some eighty years ago. It is the *'Weehavitt Shop'* today. [Anonymous, black and white printed postcard *circa* 1915, with imprint "John Macdonald, Merchant, Lochmaddy']

Lochmaddy Hotel, Lochmaddy. (D. Macfadyen, Proprietor).

126. *"Loch Maddy is at our feet and we are soon at the door of the comfortable hotel, where we find a four-course dinner, a varied wine list, sea-water baths, and fellow-guests speaking the English of the Court of King Edward VII."* You can almost feel Ada Goodrich-Freer's relief when reading these words! At last, a chance to take off ones shoes, relax, bathe, and then join ones fellow guests in the lounge of the **Lochmaddy Hotel** and discuss the events of the day in front of the open fire. Travelling through the islands was a great undertaking a century ago; a poor road surface and dangerous fords between the isles made the arrival far more enjoyable than the journey. Built in 1863, the hotel has been extended at various times and recent internal alterations should add further to the comfort of guests, and casual callers, well into the next century! [A Gaelic series, black and white printed *Cairt Phostail circa* 1902]

An advertisement for the Lochmaddy Hotel from A & C Black's 1910 handbook 'Scotland'. [Bob Charnley Collection]

The Pier, Lochmaddy, North Uist.

127. Lochmaddy Pier, departure point for the island of Harris, the subject of our next nostalgic post-card tour around the islands which will take us, ultimately, to Ness in Lewis. [Unattributed, sepia printed postcard, probably by Raphael Tuck, with the imprint 'Hugh MacDonald Ltd, Wholesale Stationers, Oban' *circa* 1939]

Shipping a Uist Pony. (Copyright.)

128. An undignified exit for the beast, but considered to be the most practical way of getting a struggling horse aboard ship at Lochmaddy pier in the 1890s. In the 1990s the animal is placed in a trailer, provided with hay and water, and driven down the ramp onto the *'Hebridean Isles';* certainly a less stressful experience. In this picture the passengers watch with amazement whilst one gentleman, on the right, fiddles with his camera. If anyone has a copy of *his* photograph please write to the publisher *now!* [A Gaelic series, black and white printed *Cairt Phostail circa* 1902, photo *circa* 1897]

A SELECT BIBLIOGRAPHY

This is a list of personal choice and I readily acknowledge the works of each author, especially if I have quoted from his or her book. Many of the titles are long out-of-print but, with the notable exception of Beveridge (£200+), they may still be found in second-hand bookshops at reasonable prices. I unhesitatingly recommend Antiquarian Bookseller, North Uist-born Domhnall MacCormaig of 19 Braid Crescent, Edinburgh EH10 6AX, telephone 0131 447 2889, email grenitote@blueyonder.co.uk. Domhnall's regular catalogues contain some fine Gaelic items, and choice books on the Highlands and Islands topography, Celtic studies and Scottish history. All enquiries to grenitote@blueyonder.co.uk.

ANDERSON, Iain F. — *'To Introduce the Hebrides' 1933*
ANDERSON, Iain F. — *'Across Hebridean Seas' 1937*
BEVERIDGE, Erskine — *"North Uist' 1911*
BLUNDELL, Dom. Odo — *'The Catholic Highlands of Scotland' 1917*
BUCHANAN, Donald — *'Reflection of the Isle of Barra' 1943 edition*
CAMPBELL, John Lorne (Ed.) — *'The Book of Barra' 1936*
CAMPBELL, John Lorne — *'Fr. Allan McDonald of Eriskay' 1954*
CHRYSTAL, Major R.A. — *'Angling at Lochboisdale' 1939*
COOPER, Derek — *'The Road to Mingulay' 1985*
CUMMING, Mrs. C.F. Gordon — *'In the Hebrides' 1883*
GOODRICH-FREER, Miss Ada — *'Outer Isles' 1902*
MACGREGOR, Alasdair Alpin — *'Behold the Hebrides' 1925*
MACGREGOR, Alasdair Alpin — *'Summer Days among the Western Isles' 1929*
MACGREGOR, Alasdair Alpin — *'Searching the Hebrides with a Camera' 1933*
MACKAY, James A. — *'The Uists and Barra - Islands Postal History Series: No.2' 1978*
MACNEIL OF BARRA, the — *'Castle in the Sea' 1964*
MACVICAR, Rev. Angus J. — *'Hebridean Heritage' 1966*
MOULD, Miss D.D.C. Pochin — *'West-Over-Sea' 1953*
MURSELL, Walter A. — *'Isles of Sunset' 1931*
REA, F.G. — *'A School in South Uist' 1964*
THOMPSON, Francis — *'Harris Tweed - The Story of a Hebridean Industry' 1969*
THOMPSON, Francis — *'The Uists and Barra' 1974*

Bob Charnley

1940 – 1999

'The Investigative Historian'

The allure of Scotland's Highlands and Islands has for centuries attracted visitors from far and wide, each captivated by the beguiling beauty of its mystical landscape. They came to witness and record the life stories of its peoples, their language, culture and traditions.

The late 19th Century saw the arrival of the 'Travelling Photographer', often employed by large agencies keen to capitalise on the booming tourism market and its associated demand for picture postcards.

Over a period of thirty years, Lancashire man, Bob Charnley diligently collected thousands of these images, producing from them a series of informative historical, postcard and photographic tour books.

Bob was educated at Stonyhurst College and St Augustine's College, County Cavan. He joined the Metropolitan Police in the early 1960's serving in central London and the Palace of Westminster. In 1968 he returned to his native county and continued his career as a detective with Lancashire Constabulary.

Utilising his skills as a detective and through tireless research, coupled with an engaging style of writing, Bob was able to bring these faded sepia prints to life, identifying often for the first time, exactly who the subjects were; and where, when and by whom they were photographed.

'Hebridean Images' is proud to be associated with 'The Bob Charnley Collection' and we acknowledge those who assisted in the production of the original editions. Our sincere and grateful thanks are extended to Mrs Sandra Charnley, in appreciation of her trust, support and friendship and for permitting us to reproduce her late husband's wonderful books.

Bob Charnley's contribution to the recording and preservation of Scottish social history is immense. His lasting legacy is that of ensuring these precious images may be accessed, understood and appreciated by future generations. He has left us with an almost tangible link to the past, of a landscape and a people captured elsewhere in time.

Frank Creighton
Hebridean Images

Books by the same author:

Joint author: